fierce

&

fabulous

Phenomenal Women in Network Marketing

fierce & fabulous

Phenomenal Women in Network Marketing

NKANDU BELTZ

National Library of Australia Cataloguing-in-Publication entry

Creator: Beltz, Nkandu, author.

Fierce and Fabulous: Phenomenal Women in Network Marketing / Nkandu Beltz.

ISBN: 9780994184788 (paperback)

Subjects:
Multilevel marketing.
Success – Anecdotes.
Self-realization in women.

Dewey Number: 658.872

Published by Author Express
www.AuthorExpress.com
publish@authorexpress.com

Dedication

To all of the women
around the world.
You have so much power
within you.
Go and unleash your
brilliance.

Nothing great happens, until someone becomes passionate about something!

My rock solid belief is ... When the WHY becomes clear, the HOW becomes easy! For the last twenty years I have travelled the world as a professional speaker showing people how to take their WHY and turn it into something that makes a difference, that is meaningful, and that matters to them and the people who mean the world to them. Their stories are so inspiring, so relatable, and so informative.

The ladies in this book are living examples of people who turned their dreams and desires into reality using the wonderful vehicle of direct marketing / network marketing. The ability to be your own boss, charter your own future, work with like minded people to guide you along the journey and have the support of leaders around so you can achieve your goals is the true essences of network marketing.

Keith Abraham
Founder, Passionate Performance Inc.

Acknowledgments

This is always the hard bit, as it takes so many people to bring a book to life. Not only with those who provide services but those who gave you the moral support to keep going.

First, I would like to acknowledge Rebecca McIntyre for asking me to curate this book. You are such an inspiration and I love your work and energy. I look forward to working with you.

My thanks go out to Debbie Loughnane and her team. Your guidance, patience, and love go a long way. Your leadership skills are great.

To all of the women featured in this book. You're all amazing, and I look forward to seeing the impact you're making.

Jacinta Petrie and Chris Kang, I'm grateful to you for working on the website and for being an amazing team.

Thank you, Fiona Jones from Author Express, for allowing me to follow in your footsteps and giving me guidance on everything related to books and publishing.

To Caryn, the writing girl. You're just amazing. Thank you for proofing this book, editing it, and making sure it's actually in English.

Narelle at NGirl Design, thank you for all the graphic designs in this book.

Many thanks to Dan Toomey, Founder and Creative Director of Style House Creative for helping to design the book cover.

To my family, Dr Erik Beltz, Michelle, Claire, and Erik Jr Beltz. You guys are so amazing. I love you. Thank you for all of the patience and love while I was working on this book during school holidays.

Last, but not least, my sincere gratitude to the divine providence for my many blessings and the gifts I have inherited.

Foreword

by Allison Mooney, CSP

It is an absolute delight and pleasure to be part of the lives and stories of these extraordinary women who show such authenticity, vulnerability, and sheer tenacity of spirit. We're all made to be inspirational, and yes, we all have potential to live fuller and exciting lives, through our businesses and personal endeavours.

Fierce and Fabulous will help us to believe more about who we are and to go for the dreams that are still inside of us. Not only will they encourage us in the "why" but also in the "how-to" in achieving one's own success.

As a professional speaker, I can tell you there were women just like that in this book who stood and walked with me – they inspired and championed me as I grew my business, and I know this book will do the same for you.

Allison Mooney, CSP
(Certified Speaking Professional)

Fewer than ten percent of the speakers who belong to the Global Speakers Federation, the body representing professional speaking associations worldwide, hold this professional designation.

CSP is the international standard they agree represents competence in the speaking profession.

Allison Mooney CSP has won **Speaker of the Year** (National Speakers Association – Auckland New Zealand) for an unprecedented third time

Allie speaks not only to the intellectual mind, but to the heart as well.

Her client list includes large organisations like, Westpac, Air New Zealand, Qantas, IAG, Toyota, Fonterra, Fuji Xerox, Drake International, Pfizer, Lufthansa Direct Selling Association. Auckland University, Harcourt Real Estate, L'Oreal Professionals, Wanganui Hospital, Goodfellow Assoc., Southern Cross Hospital, and Principals Assoc., to name a few.

Along the way she has been awarded other prestigious speaking awards

Most Inspirational Speaker 2007

Most Humorous and Entertaining Speaker in 2006 and 2008

Her best-selling book, *Pressing the Right Buttons*, earned her Author of the Year 2008 by the National Speakers Assoc. of NZ (Auck) and has been published by Random House for both Turkey and the Brazilian market.

She has spoken to over fifty-three cities around the world in the past three years.

Allie is a fun, entertaining speaker, but most important she has a message that is informative and life-changing. Her client's description... "vibrant, insightful, engaging and relevant."

ALLISON MOONEY CSP
International Professional Speaker
The People Interpreter
13 Glamorgan Drive, Torbay, Auckland, New Zealand 0630
Ph. + 64 (9) 473 6783
Mob. + 64 27 260 8532
Website www.allisonmooney.co.nz

Introduction

Welcome to *Fierce and Fabulous – Phenomenal Women in Network Marketing*.

In 2015 I published my second book, *Fierce and Fabulous-The Feminine Force of Success*. While talking to these brave and powerful women, I can't help but think about my mother, Ethel, a trained food and nutrition teacher, who worked hard to support us. When Zambia, my birth country, was going through an economic crisis, my mother uprooted her family and convinced us this was not how the story would end. She made the journey to Botswana to look for a job, so we could have an education. My mother is my perfect inspiration, and I know a lot of women who are changing the narrative to rewrite their stories.

During the process of writing this book, I did interviews with women from various vocations, from the arts and hospitality and design, to network marketing and social change. I realized these inspirational women had a message. And that message was that you can get more out of life than a dreary nine-to-five job where you work long hours and earn just enough to get by, while you line someone else's pockets. There is another way, where you can take the wheel of your own success.

Like Marianne Williamson says, "Our deepest fear is not that we are inadequate. Our deepest fear is that we are powerful beyond measure. It's our light, not our darkness, that most frightens us. We ask ourselves, 'Who am I to be brilliant, gorgeous, talented and fabulous?' Actually, who are you NOT to be?"

My Experience with Network Marketing

I was curious about network marketing, and after having had a few conversations with Rebecca McIntyre, I began to understand why she was so passionate about network marketing and wanted to know how I could play a part in it. I know that the best way to create a legacy and help others is by helping yourself first.

In the past, network marketing was seen as a hobby for stay-at-home mums drinking coffee while eating finger foods. Network marketing has come a long way since the 50's where people are now able to run multimillion-dollar business. This is far from the truth these days. What I've found is that this industry generates billions of dollars. The top ten Network Marketing companies from the Direct Selling Association last year companies all generated over one billion dollar revenue a year world wild. .

Network marketing promotes entrepreneurship and start-up requires little capital. It's dependent on effort and not position. This means there are no politics. Nobody gets ahead unless they put in the work. It's also important to note that recruiting is important but not a requirement, as income is also generated through sales of products and services.

Direct selling is not a new concept. In network marketing, you can make money by selling products directly to consumers as well as building your own sales organizations and receiving commissions or bonuses on the sales generated by the distributors in the organizations.

As Stephen R. Covey says in *The 7 Habits of Highly Effective Marketing Professionals*: "Effective network marketers have a clear vision and passion for that vision. They know what they want to achieve where they see themselves in their business organization. Everything they do, every activity they perform, is driven by that vision."

Having spent some time with these women, I found that I was intrigued, and my perception shifted. I discovered that the people who weren't afraid of what others thought of them did very well. I also found some key common elements in all of these women.

1. The amount of confidence is just infectious. These women are determined. They encourage each other and help everyone succeed.

2. They have skills that include sales and implementation. These are women in business, and they go about it in a classy and sophisticated manner.

3. They have peace of mind. This comes from knowing they will have residual income for a very long time.

4. They enjoy in their lives.

5. They all seem to be well travelled.

6. They have improved personal relationships and seem to have a balanced life in all areas.

7. They invest in personal growth.

I'm a firm believer in investing in you. By doing so, you will also help others to grow. I remember watching Oprah Winfrey talking with Robert Kiyosaki. I didn't understand what it was all about, but I wanted to know why some people could make so much money. It's all about mentality and changing the way you think. Many women have walked the path of success through network marketing, but looking at these women who are flourishing in their lives, persuaded me to share their stories.

This book has been written for people who are looking to get more out of life. If by reading this book you only get one message, let it be that you alone have the power to change your destiny and the lives of people around you. This business has worked for those bold and brave enough to step up and give it a go.

With love and gratitude,

Nkandu Beltz

Invictus

Out of the night that covers me,

Black as the Pit from pole to pole,

I thank whatever gods may be

For my unconquerable soul.

In the fell clutch of circumstance

I am the master of my fate:

I am the captain of my soul.

William Earnest Henley

Contents

"If you build it, they will come."

Kevin Costner as Ray
Kinsella, Field of Dreams

❧

CHAPTER 1

Debbie Loughnane

Debbie Loughnane

What is your background?

In high school I moved to the country with my family, as they wanted a different lifestyle. I liked the pace and the people, and the close proximity to the city. However, growing up in a small country town of about six-thousand people I realised work opportunities were limited, unless you wanted to travel to the city. I thought I would move back to the city when I was older, but the country is where I met my husband, Tim, and we raised our two daughters, Emily and Tayla.

I left home at a young age and was independent at seventeen years old. I had a full-time job and did lots of different side jobs, from being a freelance fitness instructor, to a freelance makeup artist, to then opening my own fashion boutiques when I was in my twenties. I loved seeing people feel good about themselves. They'd walk in feeling ordinary and walk out feeling fabulous. I had that business for thirteen years, but after ten years I started to think differently about life. In 2005 I lost my beautiful mum, who I watched work herself into the ground, and at that time I remember thinking, *Is this all there is?* I wanted to show my daughters the best of life, and I remember being so flat, defeated, and down after losing my mum. It was like there was a big hole in my heart, and I felt empty. I kept thinking there had to be more to life and kept asking, "Okay, so now what?"

On the surface I seemed to have it all together, but underneath I was struggling financially and didn't have that peace of mind and fulfilment I longed for. I started to look at different opportunities, from creating my own jewellery line or fashion label, to expanding my image consulting business that was attached to my boutique. I wanted to teach and inspire people in a big way that there was more to life and we can live an extraordinary life.

Do you know how many people lack confidence in the way they dress or apply makeup? Personal presentation stops people sometimes from stepping outside of their comfort zone and feeling empowered. Most people hide in their shell but secretly want more. It's unfortunate they don't know where to start. I knew this instinctively. Yes, I could have expanded what I knew and grown that part of the business, but to be honest I was exhausted and felt like I was driving myself mad with trying to find a better solution to improve my life and hone my skills. That's when network marketing changed everything. I was able to bring what I knew into my network marketing business and inspire people to choose more for themselves.

How did you get into network marketing?

I received an email in 2007 that began to change my life, as well as the lives of millions of others around the world. But at the time, I didn't know the impact it would have for me to be a forward thinker and take my life in my hands.

Sometimes an opportunity knocks once, or maybe twice, and I'd had a few opportunities in my life that didn't feel quite right for me. I truly believe that being presented an opportunity is all about the correct fit for you, personally and professionally. I remember being offered this kind of business in different forms over the years, but I didn't have a connection with the company, the awesome people, or the products.

With this incredible company, I could see the big picture. My heart skipped a beat. My mind started spinning, and my gut feeling was so strong that I never had a doubt! I was understandably impressed, because this business model was taught at Harvard Business School. The compensation plan also appeared to be one of the best I'd ever seen. The history, foundations, rewards, and the spirit of generosity of this company blew me away. All I needed to do was take that first leap of faith and seek to actively change my professional life, personal wellbeing, and income status. No one was going to do it for me. I felt like I had to take charge instead of being a person who complained about my circumstances. I felt alive. I always say that if it's meant to be, it's up to me. The excitement and creativity started to flow. I could see the possibilities for the first time in a long time, instead of the limitations of letting my ego say no.

Prior to joining this incredible industry, I had no experience in network marketing, and my confidence in myself was low. I was not a public speaker, nor did I have any prior experience in running a business like this. I did have an entrepreneurial spirit that made me want to tap into something grand and harness the skills I did have. These skills were people-based. I just love people and seeing the smile on their faces from the belief they have in themselves when their confidence grows due to whatever they're learning, feeling, or experiencing. Some people have never been recognised or gifted anything in their lives, and I wanted to be part of that feeling and pay it forward. To change people's lives by being a generous leader and making someone's day, year, and life.

As I grew up, I watched my mum run herself into the ground at an early age working two jobs, and thought that was the norm. The focus was on getting a good job, buying a house, having kids, and retiring at the end of your work life career. I felt like it was a predictable movie that was like everyone else's, and I craved more. It was like a longing inside of me. A void that needed to be filled. A cup that was empty.

I couldn't fathom being away from my girls that much and not being present in their lives. My grandmother had pretty much been the same, and I knew that being a mother of two girls, I didn't want them to think once you receive the cards you were dealt, it meant you had to live the rest of your life with the same, old same old. As a conscious parent, I wanted to show my two daughters there were more possibilities in life.

So, once I experienced the vehicle of network marketing and knowing this was a legitimate business, the history of the company, along with the vision of the founder and incredible products that were unique in their own right, I knew in my heart of hearts this was totally for me. And not only me, but thousands, if not millions, of people who were in the same exact boat as I was. And if I could just go for it and take that first leap of faith, others would see what I could see.

I knew that not everyone would join me. Some would and some wouldn't, but I also knew that ninety-seven percent of people earned under $150,000 per year, and they were not prepared to do what the three percent were willing to, which was to stretch out of their comfort zone, aim for targets, and create a bright, happy, and positive future, because they cared more about what people thought of them than how they could pay the bills and inspire others to break the mould.

With my network marketing business, I could walk away from a business that was carrying a big debt. After thirteen years, I knew nothing was going to change unless I said yes to my gut feeling and yes to this opportunity that would be the transformer for me and my family, as well as millions around me.

I was the person who had NO TIME or had NO MONEY, so this business was the perfect fit for me, because I actually had nothing to lose. I was on the edge emotionally and financially. I worked this business around a full-time business and family. I was like a sponge. I learned all I could as quickly as I could, and took as much action as I could. My vision was so big, I could see the possibilities. I jumped in with both feet not knowing a thing, and was able to replace my income from my fashion boutique within four months. Then I closed the doors and walked away. I even did a happy dance!

I knew then and there I could take it further. Back then, it was a part-time effort alongside my current situation. I understood where I could be if I allocated more time and energy into growing the foundations of this network marketing business.

The most awesome thing is that I was excited for the first time in a long time, and I felt ignited. I knew the person who'd sent me that email was earning more in a month than I had in a year, and that no matter how hard I worked and how many stores I opened, my life was that treadmill, and I was getting off!

My motto is that we have one shot at life, and we can make the best of what we have when we're the creator of our own reality. We can be, do, and have more, but we need a vehicle, and I'd been looking my whole life for that vehicle, until it landed in my lap as a network marketing business.

When I started my network marketing business, my daughters were ten and fourteen. My husband had been at the same job for twenty-eight years. I'd heard about other women who'd retired their husbands with this business, and I knew he'd supported me throughout the years with my harebrained schemes of opening several businesses and always struggling. It was like he believed that if I set my mind to something, it would be created.

Traditional business comes with all of the overheads, long hours, and capital required to start up and stay afloat. After thirteen years in the game, I was tired. Tired of not getting anywhere or even feeling like I had a life. A dream is only a wish if you never take action, and I knew serious action was required.

As I said, within four months I'd replaced my income working this business around my full-time boutique, and I could walk away. Within a year I earned the first car on the road for the company. I now have over forty white Mercedes Benzes on the road, because I said yes, and the leaders to follow could see my vision and feel my passion. We've attracted people from all walks of life into our business without any prior experience in this industry. Here's a snapshot of the leaders' backgrounds in our organisation:

- Men and women

- Gen Y's to retirement age

- Doctors

- Pharmacists

- Accountants

- Makeup artists

- Beauty therapists

- Hairdressers franchise and business owners

- Lawyers

- Veterinarians

- Teachers

- Financial planners

- Professional athletes

- Nutritionists and naturopaths

- Fitness professionals

- Stay-at-home mums and dads

- People looking to replace or create a six-figure income

Just to name a few.

My two incredible daughters are in the business with me. Emily is in this book and will share her story. She's the youngest Regional Vice President in Australia, a Gen Y earning her six figure income and driving her beautiful white Mercedes. My other daughter, Tayla, just turned eighteen and joined us in the business, as she didn't want to miss out on all of the fun. She saw our old life and our new one.

My husband was able to walk away from his tradie job of twenty-eight years and be there to support me. He now gets to go fishing and do what he loves on a daily basis, instead of feeling the pressure to bring home the weekly wage handed to him. I love the relationships and lifelong friends he's made with our team. The guys are down-to-earth men who just want to support their partners and live an extraordinary life

I never thought at the beginning I would be the top income earner in our company or the first person in Australia to be in the Leadership Council or top thirteen income earner worldwide, or earn the incentive trips that were up for grabs. Being a sole trader in my old life, I can tell you there was none of that. And now I get to strive personally and professionally every day to raise the bar and show others that extraordinary is only where you see it to be, and the possibilities are endless.

How did you have the courage to say yes to that email from the other side of the world?

When I look back now, I think about how much my mind was constantly trying to figure out what was next for me and my family. I was bored out of my brain. There were no more challenges, no more highlights, no more fun, no more excitement, but to be honest, I wasn't willing to risk money or time on something that wasn't proven successful and were time and money-consuming.

When I was offered this opportunity I now know is the most incredibly rewarding thing anyone could ever do, at the time I had a few doubts. It was starting from scratch and building it up. But I had no direction anyway, so I had nothing to lose and only loads to gain personally and professionally. I spoke with my dad, because that small voice of doubt was there. My heart was pulling me to a yes, and my logical mind was saying no.

When I spoke with my dad, he gave me encouragement. His advice to me was from a line in the movie, *Field of Dreams* with Kevin Costner. He said "Build it, and they will come." His voice keeps playing over and over in my head whenever doubt set in, especially in the beginning when I was flying blind. Now, when I attend our annual company global conferences and events I put on for our organisation, I actually have tears in my eyes when I see the amount of faces whose lives have changed, because I did "build it," and they came.

So I made that conscious choice then and there that network marketing was a no-brainer. People have skin and hair, the world is moving fast with the Internet, and this business ticked every box for me to be able to empower, inspire, and teach others to either use the products or join me in building a team and create an online multimillion-dollar business without overheads, massive capital, or start-up costs.

I had not one thing to lose except if I gave up or didn't see the potential and work on teaching people about the business opportunity or the botanical products. I couldn't afford not to seriously look at this business and make it work for me by being the evidence, so I could not only inspire others to join my team but show people that the company and industry actually is incredible if you create it that way…or don't! But being the evidence is the proof people need to see as to how, why, and what works.

Ninety-seven percent of people don't have the courage to think outside of the box and take action, yet they complain constantly about their life. Other people's points of view were not going to pay my bills or reduce the debt I'd incurred in my business. When you have an open heart and mind, anything is possible. Anything can be achieved. It's about taking the first step, and then the next, and then the next. Don't look at all of the steps. Just take one at a time. It takes more energy to live in fear, doubt, and limitation than it does to come from creativity, fun, and joy.

Before I said yes to a complete stranger, who is now one of my best friends, I first researched the company, had several conversations, experienced the products, and most of all, I trusted in my gut that I call my inner guidance system. It had never failed me before, and I knew this was my next chapter of fun, travel, growth, peace of mind and to build lifelong friends with like-minded people walking the same path.

How has your network marketing business changed your life?

This industry has transformed my whole life in more ways than I could ever imagine. Like that movie *Groundhog Day* where he lived the same day over and over. Every day I tried to convince myself it was going to get better and more fun, and I would earn more money and pay off my debt one day. That was my old life. Even though I enjoyed my clients, being in the fashion industry, and wearing nice clothes, that was all there was until I asked for more.

So, now my days now are different. I can just take off for a week to the beach. Work my business from anywhere. Go overseas on holidays I've achieved, paid for by my company, and have long lunches and awesome conversations. The ability to buy simple things like a coffee, have my nails done, learn more at personal development courses, and build my leadership skills, so I can share that inspiration and pay it forward.

There isn't one day that's the same as the next. There's always something to bounce out of bed for, such as a trip, meeting, conference, training, or promotion. I've travelled to more places than I had before, so here's a little snapshot of old and new travel experiences.

Old travel experiences:

Queensland and one O/S trip to Bali. My typical holiday came with stress and pressure due to lack of funds. I needed a break but couldn't afford it very often. We had a timeshare week we used every two years to go to Queensland or the country. Pretty boring, really, and uninspiring to say the least.

New travel experiences:

Once per year I now get to travel to Las Vegas for our annual Global Conference and Local Interstate Conference for Australia. I've had incentive trips every year to these awesome five-seven star destinations with my family to Hayman Island, Fiji, Broome, Port Douglas, Hawaii, and Queensland. At the top level of the company, all National Vice Presidents and a guest are invited to Maui in January. I've been there about six times. Other incentive trips at this level are to beautiful, exotic locations for me and my husband to Prague, Vienna, Budapest, Rome, Tuscany, and Florence for the top achievers in the company. We also have a local incentive promotion for elevating incentives for promoting direct leaders in the business. These have been to Sydney, Barossa Valley, Uluru, New Zealand, and many more.

Who inspires you, and why?

Oprah, Anthony Robbins, Sandy Forster, Will smith, Jim Carey, Michael McQueen, Keith Abraham, Allison Mooney and Nkandu Beltz, because they're thought leaders.

My husband, Tim, and my two daughters Emily and Tayla, are my inspirations and biggest supporters, because they can also see my vision for us and are in total appreciation of my beliefs and dreams. They've seen firsthand how life can be beautiful if you follow through on a dream and achieve what you set out to do.

My stellar rockstar team. My frontline NVPs, Angela Weston, Sanja Jovanovic, Nicole Chugg and Rebecca McIntyre. My direct RVPs, Emily Loughnane, Suzanne Nanos, Chelsea Dolby and Jacqui Way. My direct managers, Gina Charos, Regan Kennedy, Michelle Ryan, Michelle James, Michelle Fellows, and Julie Ryan. All of the NVPs, RVPs and managers /

leaders within my successline. They inspire me every day to be their shining light, as they are mine. My beautiful sponsor Christy is owed a big thank you for breathing life into me. I don't know where I would be without all of them walking beside me.

Believe it or not, the people who are content with their lives, but complain, inspire me to show others what's possible to break the mould, create the extraordinary, be the invitation for change, and breathe life into those willing to receive the gifts of choice and possibility. These complaining people inspire me, because I see how I don't want to be or live.

I'm inspired by other leaders in network marketing who have incredible stories. They're the true pioneers. I'm inspired by other people's energy. I'm not talking about pushy or aggressive people, but those who have a presence you're instantly drawn too.

I'm inspired by my team. By the leadership they bring to the organization. Each of them has a story in this book and didn't have a network marketing story when they started. They carved out their future and partnered with me and their sponsor to be extraordinary. Their open heart and mind, and the way they think outside of the box, shows me they're courageous to not be the norm.

I remember in my fashion stores and image consultancy businesses that I had a thirst for personal development and empowerment to just make someone else feel special, beautiful, and important. I would read ferociously books by Robert Kioysaki, Sandy Forster, Wayne Dyer, and Ester and Jerry Hicks, as well as books on leadership and building big business that were duplicable. But then I remember thinking, *Okay so now what?*

I had a shop. I could do business, but I was getting the same results and not moving forward. I had to create something, make something, or have a brilliant idea and apply those principles. But I was exhausted from being everything to everyone, standing on my feet nine hours a day constantly thinking how I could grow my business.

I even opened a second store, trying to be entrepreneurial, but that wasn't twice the profit, only twice the overheads and headaches. So when it came to being offered this business and what the monthly income potential could be. I nearly fell off the chair, as I was earning that in a year, not a month.

I saw everyday people could create an extraordinary lifestyle and be a top earner if they were willing to put the time into development as leaders and business professionals, and to keep going and work on themselves to become a master in the industry. You can earn an extra $500 - $5,000-plus or be an incredible difference-maker in the world. It's about the people, the freedom, fun, and the flexibility. As I'm writing this, I'm on a trip to a beach location I've been to five times this year. It's my happy place I go to just to have a little downtime.

Because I love this business so much, I get sheer joy from creating and being with people who are transforming their lives, and the lives of others, doing what the three percent are not willing to do. I felt like I had to take charge instead of being a person who complained about my circumstances.

When we start to entertain the idea of a network marketing business, our mind can play a game of doubt and ego, and perceive things that may or may not be true. We worry about what our friends, family, and others will think. Will they be a part of this idea? Will they support me?

We start to make up stories in our own head to talk ourselves out of seeing it through, in case someone thinks less of us. For me I had no one to impress, talk into, or convince. I just did it anyway. As the Bon Jovi song says, "Like Frankie said, I did it my way." I didn't question my choice once I decided, because I knew it was proven. I knew I would see it through. I knew I would go the distance. I knew it worked. I didn't know how, but I just kept going one step at a time.

What are the main attributes you feel have helped you the most to be successful in the industry?

I have a high internal drive to make anything work that I set my mind to. I know I can make it happen, it just comes down to the skills that need to be learnt along the way.

It's about total alignment in mindset. If I don't know something, I'll learn about it and develop any skills required to make it happen. I've learnt what I needed to regarding everything relevant to the business. I had a hunger that needed to be fed. I truly believe that if we work on ourselves and give it a hundred percent, then it will happen. I'm not afraid of hard work. My will is so strong. I have a sense of knowing to follow the energy of what's next for me and the team, to be on the ball with current information, and to be innovative.

I've seen so many people in this industry, prior to me joining it, giving it a bad name and ruining it for others. They could blame their upline company and others as to why it didn't work, but deep in my soul I wanted to show people that it does work if you create the evidence. It creates the proof it doesn't matter where you come from, it's how you go about it.

How much credibility do you have with what you do now? How do you leave people when you meet up with them? Do you leave them still wanting more, or do they feel pushed and bullied into joining? I teach my team to never convince anyone. I'm the evidence. If I didn't want this to work, I wouldn't have had that spark inside of me. That fire. I invest in me all of the time, even with being at the top of the company. I'm still learning, growing, creating, and being inspired to be a better version of myself

I also knew that my sponsor had started in a small country town of six-thousand people and had another leader in her town at the top of the company. If that was the case, then why would this not work for me? They were my evidence. My role models. They were where my vision started to grow. Even though they were on the other side of the world, I knew anything was possible if I took the actual steps to make it work. Not one day did I ever treat my business like a hobby. I was the CEO and the creator of my future. Either way I chose it to work. My mind was spinning with ideas, and I actually took action.

See, most people have million-dollar ideas and don't implement any of them. Then they wonder why, when they thought of this person or that person, but they just let opportunities slip by. Put enough energy into anything, and it will be created. Think of a house you're building or a wedding you're planning. You don't really want to do an ordinary job, do you? NO! Then why wouldn't you take this more seriously and go for it with all of your might and work on the areas that aren't working? Be open to coaching, learning, and growing, and ask how you can be a better leader and business owner.

I remember bugging my sponsor. I never let up about what I needed to do or learn in order to become a world-class leader, but also to duplicate that. We're only as good as the leaders we develop, so I was relentless in my learning to be that leader for my team. An excellent leader will ask loads of questions and be willing to be coachable and open to suggestions, though it may not be what we want to hear sometimes. I was grateful for, and of, my upline's time. It was so valuable, and I never took it, or her, for granted. I had total respect for her and her time and wanted others to value mine.

I also knew I had to get this done as quickly as possible, and at times I didn't have access to information I needed to make me grow. But instead of being the victim, I went and sourced it. I adopted coaches and went to courses and read. I listened to podcasts and CDs and chose to become a master of the network marketing industry. Tony Robbins has said that if you spend enough time in an industry doing and learning, you will become a master, and you will only expand from there. I can now pay it forward with my knowledge and mentoring.

What were the biggest hurdles you had overcome to get where you are today?

Starting from scratch in a country that had no foundations to build upon was my biggest hurdle. Having an upline in another country. The huge time difference. Not having any leadership to follow or partner, and no system in place. All of these are needed to build an empire, and these are the foundations that have to be created in order to have a system for others to follow, believe in, and duplicate.

I had no documents, no events, and no system to plug people into. I spent years developing these. I had a vision. I didn't want others to feel the same as I did, so I partnered a couple of my incredibly talented leaders, and we fumbled our way through to create our system the way it is today. We stay on top of changes together.

We have a team culture, which is that we are one, and we protect that by keeping it simple and streamlined with a professional edge. I wanted our team to feel like they were safe and at home in our environment. To feel they could leave politics at the door and be surrounded by business professionals who chose a productive environment that developed leadership in everyone in the organisation, so they could plug into the events, trainings and calls.

Every one of us starts at the same level. This business is a level playing field, and for those who are willing to go the distance, we can, and will, create the extraordinary. But it's up to us to stay the course, invest time into developing ourselves as leaders/entrepreneurs, and do the income-producing activity that's required to build that multimillion-dollar business.

Treat it like a hobby, and that's what you will get. It's that simple. We don't buy a million-dollar franchise to only show up when we feel like it or when the stars have aligned NO! We go in, we work hard, we do everything from mopping the floors to taking out the trash, and build those foundations in ourselves and our business.

Network marketing is not just about flitting around having coffees. It's about building relationships and seeing who's on the same page and is a resonant match for you and your business. But if you don't get out of the house, they won't come knocking on your door, or call you to join, or order your product.

I think the misconception is that it will just come to you if you put in a few minutes a day. I promise you that if you can make some adjustments in your life regarding what doesn't serve you and put time into your business, you will get out of it what you put into it. I teach my team and daughters that you reap what you sow. That means you need to plant the best crop, water it constantly, and sprinkle your energy, kindness, and time into others if they meet you halfway. Value your time, and work with those who do what they say. Remember, watch what people do, not what they say.

If you were able to start all over again, what would you do differently?

In the early stages I had a lot of success by company and personal measures. But there were times when I lost momentum due to trying to create systems and documents and manage my team, rather than building more direct leaders.

I spent a lot of energy with the wrong people. I wasted so much family time on the people who said they wanted it but didn't, because they would always look to me for why they weren't where they wanted to be. I was their source, and they needed to be their own source. I'm more than happy to mentor and coach my leaders, but when they make more excuses than taking action, it's an uphill battle.

I remember a mentor once said to me, "Deb, you can't light a flame if there's no spark." That's when I let go. I was holding on way too tightly, and they were taking my time and energy. They just wanted to feed off me and hang out, so they kept saying what I wanted to hear, and I kept hearing what I wanted to hear. So I let go. I now teach my team that I can lead them to water, but I can't make them drink. I guess my biggest piece of advice is to value your time more than anything. It's easy to be sucked into the vortex of other people's wants and needs, but when you value your time, so will others.

I also believe I overcompensated, because my sponsor was not here in Australia, so I decided to be a martyr and be everything I could be. Just pick your people well. Remember, you will be going on holidays with these leaders, and if they're opposed to hard work, they can impact your life and your existing team. Get to know people, and build strong relationships with them.

I also make sure my leaders know they have to text me during business hours if they need anything. I created boundaries with my time and phone, and that has been incredible. It creates total respect, and also this will be duplicated throughout your entire organisation. Remember, what you do, your team will do. The culture of positivity and authenticity is key, so make sure nothing comes back to haunt you. From day one, think about how you choose to operate your business. I made just as many mistakes with my time, but not with culture, authenticity, and credibility

What was it like to be one of the first people in Australia to start with the company? How did you have the vision to create what you have?

The word *evidence* is a big one to me I had to create something of myself in order to smile again, and the evidence had to be big.

From the bottom of my heart, I wanted to be a difference-maker in the industry. I know our company is full of heart, and the foundation the company culture was built upon was created by our founder, so that it flows right through all of the incredible leaders before me. It wasn't just another company. It was new to Australia but proven in the USA, and I knew I had the chance to bring all of that here and paint the same vision to others of what was painted for me. For the first time, my eyes were opened, and I had a light that would not go out. I wanted to be an inspiration.

My two daughters are both in the business with me. I wrote on a piece of paper when they were little girls that my dream was to one day have our own multimillion-dollar business together. When they both saw me as the happiest mum they know, that's when I realised I'd inspire them to be, do, and have more, and also be incredible role models. When they asked to join, it was the happiest day in my career. That to me is the evidence right there. When they decide to be part of it, because they'd witnessed it themselves.

Our children are a product of their environment, and I'm so grateful I was offered this business and said yes. Even if my daughters set their minds to more creative endeavours, they will have the confidence to know they can do anything, because this is the motto in our home. They're listening to personal development, and this information is being imprinted onto them. The positivity and skills that the parents are listening to and learning, have a major impact on their children's lives.

A Japanese Researcher, Dr Masaru Emotto, did a study about our body being made up over seventy-percent water. He took water crystals from around the world. With music and words as a vibration, he could visibly see under a microscope, that the crystals had formed into beautiful and unique shapes. This all happened due to positive words of love, joy, encouragement, classical music, and then with different types of sounds. He's also done studies with children in classrooms where they wrote happy, positive words on jars of water. They stayed pure, clean, and clear, while the other jar had negative words, and the water went brown and murky. The water had come from the same source. With regard to the molecular structure of water, our intent (thoughts), words, ideas, and music, have a profound healing or destructive effect on it.

Since humans are seventy-percent water, ultimately it means that what we think creates our reality, not just emotionally but physically. Since the planet is also seventy-percent water, these experiments have profound implications for the environment as well. Could this mean we could 'think' a polluted stream clean again?

So, I'm so happy we're in this together and that my children are surrounded by the greatest teachers of life, while being two of the greatest role model for others. I also wanted to show my girls that if you work at it, the rewards are extraordinary, and they, too, can have a lifestyle business that will be passed on for generations. Before my mum passed away, she'd worked so hard all of her life, and it was hard watching her. If my mum were alive today, I could take care of her and give her peace of mind.

I wanted to show my girls proof that an opportunity like this is worth pursuing, so you can also pursue other dreams and passions. Building a network marketing business gives you total freedom to choose so much more in your life. Put the time in at the beginning, build your leaders, breathe life into others, be the source of inspiration and information, and enjoy seeing others' development by your mentoring and guidance. Let go of those who are not willing to go the distance with you, because that's okay. That's their choice, and they're happy making excuses rather than living an abundant life.

You've created the most amazing organization. How have you maintained such a fantastic culture within your team?

When I had my boutiques, I had a great culture there. It was a small team that worked alongside me, and they felt valued and appreciated. Staff stayed with me for a long time. I was easygoing and flexible, but they knew I had a standard and modelled that behaviour. They intuitively knew what I expected of them, as they were representing me.

So when I looked at this business, I knew it was going to be much larger than that. People would join if they felt safe, uplifted, and inspired, even if they weren't go-getters as such. They were there to be a better person. To learn and build confidence and skills. Many have said to me, "I feel like home when I'm with you."

I believe people come into a business like network marketing because of the invitation for fun and flexibility, to learn and earn, and to create an abundant life all round. I absolutely love the company's generous spirit and how they reward and gift us on multiple occasions throughout the year just for doing what we love.

I wanted to create that same spirit of generosity within our team culture and teach people about gifting and receiving. Did you know some people had never even been given a piece of jewellery before or received a bunch of flowers? I LOVE spoiling my leaders and watching their faces light up, because I've given them a heartfelt gift. I teach this right throughout our team, and it's duplicated well at all levels. I'm so proud to see this spirit paid forward.

People also choose network marketing, because they want to leave corporate politics behind. Our teams are trained by me, over and over again, about ethics culture and how to build a big, beautiful business. My direct leaders then duplicate that out. Trust and integrity are high on my values, and we can only be the best role models for our team. We can only teach them what our organisation is about, and it's up to them to follow through and create the same environment that is like-minded and ONE! We come together often and bring out the best in each other. We educate them on how to be the best version of themselves and how to attract like-minded people, and let go of those who have a different agenda.

I teach them to always go to their upline for support and never dump on their team. To be the person who won't ever say a bad word about anyone and stay true to that, even if they don't agree with their point of view. I tell them not to try so hard to be liked. To just be okay with who they are. It's not a popularity contest. It's okay to just be you and change the world one person at a time.

What does the future look like for Debbie Loughnane?

I feel at peace with my future, knowing I've build four direct National Vice Presidents to the top level at this point and have many more directs in the making. Only a small number of people have done this over the company's thirty-five years, but I'm actually showing others within my team, and the greater company, that it is possible if you stay the course, keep the drama at bay, and be the best role model for your team and others. Be the evidence that it works from anywhere if you're willing to work on yourself more than wasting time.

People say at this level, with four direct NVPs, that I can go to the beach and never have to maintain the multimillion-dollar business. But for me I've only just started. I'm excited about going to the beach when I want to, as I now do many times a year, but the best thing is that there are still so many more lives to change. I want to be their inspiration and light and show them there is a better choice

My husband was able to walk away from a job of twenty-eight years as a tradie, and he now travels with me and helps me out more at home, which gives me the opportunity to stay connected to my greater team.

Quite a few years back now, I was able to say, "Love, you don't have to work anymore at your job. You've supported me all of our lives together, and you can go do whatever you like, whenever you like." This was one of the highlights of my life. To see the peace on his face. To know I'd gifted him that, because of his belief and unconditional love for me, and his support in the business. He says. "It's all the work behind the scenes" and jokes that I'm a harder boss than his old one.

We've now been able to purchase investment properties to build our wealth and portfolio that we could never do before. We've put an extension on our home I call the "Princess Wing." We travel at least five times a year, both international and domestic.

I also have plans to have a home at the beach sometime soon.

My future is about health and learning. I plan on partnering and promoting more direct leaders who are willing to be the best version of themselves to be mentored by me personally, while still staying in touch and doing what I do best, and that's being around people and bringing out the best in them.

I want to concentrate on being a difference-maker and creating a foundation with my family. Our dream is to impact others less fortunate than we are and to give back. That's what excites me the most.

What are your top tips for success in network marketing?

1. BE A ROLE MODEL.

    Be everything you say you want to be. Choose to be that evidence for your team as a role model in personal activity, and create a beautiful culture for your team. It starts with you, and only you. Be the best leader on your team. Be the evidence that if you work on yourself and are in personal activity, you will gain the respect of your team. No one wants you to ride their coattails and manage them without contributing to your own business. They can see it, and they know it. Go the extra mile for your working leaders and give them your best asset, which is time.

2. STAY TRUE TO WHO YOU ARE.

    Remember that whatever you do, duplicates. Stay humble and approachable and kind and generous, and be careful not to get too ahead of yourself and check in with yourself. At times you will receive a lot of recognition, and I've seen people change in an interesting way because of it. Sometimes they start bouncing around like they're the be all and end all. Give someone you love permission to let you know the truth, and take it on board. This will be part of leadership growth, and it can be a phase.

3. BE OPEN TO LEARNING.

    Ask your uplines, or someone you know who's more successful than you are, how you can you can be a better leader, and be open to learning what that is. You may not like what you hear, and it's not easy to receive, but it's one of the best ways an upline can mentor you on your own personal development. Be willing to learn, as long as it's delivered in a kind and caring manner to nurture your development.

Be willing to sponsor up. That means people who are more confident more and connected are go-getters. Learn from them and do this together. Be okay that others have better skills than you do. Build the Board of Directors you want to represent your organisation. Let go of those who are wasting your time, and only take advice from people more successful than you are.

People want to share their personal experience of network marketing and rain on your parade. They don't want you to succeed, because then they'll realise they failed. Only you can decide if you will be a success, and your actions and mindset will determine that. Be okay with their point of view. My dad could have dissuaded me, but he didn't. He said, "Build it, and they will come." Surround yourself with like-minded people and be okay with losing those relationships that no longer serve and support you, because you will grow personally and professionally, and they won't.

There will be times when some relationships are toxic, and you may not have seen it in the past, but will in the future. Everyone has a choice as to how they choose to live, so be a hundred percent confident with your choices and follow through to the greatest rewards of your life. It's not just about money but about personal growth and a sense of contribution to others. That, my friends, is ABUNDANCE!

4. CONSISTENCY IS EVERYTHING.

I've been consistent from day one and followed through on all things team-related. They knew I was their rock, and that even if their upline wasn't there, I was, and I would have training events they could plug into and grow, as well as plug their developing teams into. My suggestion is to read, learn, and go to every event to build your belief. Develop yourself.

Take it on as an apprenticeship and become master at your own network marketing business

5. BE THE VAULT

Be the person everyone knows that if they share something with you, it stays with you. But also be clear you're not the solution. You're a mentor and a support for them. Keep it business-related. We're not marriage councillors, so know it's okay to tell them they need to seek professional help, since it's outside of your skill base.

Also have boundaries, so people don't make you a dumping ground for their problems. Ask them to give you five minutes on the topic, and then ask them a question that helps them find a solution for themselves. We don't have to always solve problems. We just need to learn how to lead and be present with each person.

My Message for you:

I know the stories you are about to read are so beautiful and inspiring, and my dream for you is that you now have the flame inside of you that creates a burning desire to choose something incredible for yourself! Its time for you to smile and dream again. Dream! Believe! Achieve!

Thank you,

Deb xx

Don't ever let somebody tell you, you can't do something. Not even me. All right? You got a dream, you gotta protect it. People can't do something themselves, they wanna tell you, you can't do it. If you want something, go get it. Period.

Will Smith as Chris Gardner,
Pursuit of Happyness

CHAPTER 2

Rebecca McIntyre

CHAPTER TWO

Rebecca McIntyre

What is your background?

My name is Rebecca McIntyre, and I'm happily married to my husband, Brent. We have an eight-year-old daughter named Izabella, and we live in a small, rural city with a population of 18,000. I've lived there my whole life and enjoyed a fantastic childhood.

Sport was my priority in life for about thirteen years. I played high-level basketball as a junior and absolutely loved being a part of several teams throughout my younger years. My dad said at my twenty first that sport was the best parent I had.

During my time playing basketball, I learned so many skills that have served me well in my adult life. I set goals early and worked hard to achieve them. I was disciplined and dedicated to my goal. My parents were hardworking people who sacrificed a lot for me to be able to compete at such high levels. A lot of the time they didn't have the money to put me through the camps, travel, and equipment I needed, but I never missed out. I didn't realise at the time what a massive impact it would have on how I would be as an adult and parent, and they probably didn't, either.

One time I needed basketball shoes, and I listened in when my mum and dad talked about how they couldn't afford them. My dad said he wouldn't have that. I would have the best, and he'd work overtime to get them. I don't think they knew I was listening, but this shaped me as a person and also as a giver. I learnt early on from my selfless parents that when you give to others, you will receive that back five-fold. I also learnt to be grateful and respectful to them, and I never took anything for granted. These early lessons shaped my work ethic and all of the values and morals I have as an adult.

My dad went on to run a successful company for many years and showed me if you work hard enough to achieve your dream, you can get whatever you want.

In sport, I learnt how to sacrifice. I didn't have a life other than basketball from when I was twelve until eighteen. I had some amazing achievements, most of them because of my dad's commitment and support. When I was fourteen I played for the Dandenong rangers for two years, and my dad used to take a day off work and travel to Melbourne with me every Friday. I knew they couldn't afford for him not to work, but they survived and did whatever it took, because it was my dream.

The drive took five hours, because back then there was no tunnel in Melbourne. I'd play on the Friday, we would stay the night, and I would train with team the next day before we drove home. We did this for two years, because my dad knew it was how I'd become a better player. Again, this showed me how to do whatever it takes to get to where you're going. Also, that living in the country didn't have to affect my abilities or dreams. Skills and lessons I will be forever grateful for.

From my sporting days, I've continued to have so many amazing memories and lifelong friends. I understand that no individual is bigger than the team and that you always put the team first before yourself. These are invaluable lessons I've adapted to my network marketing business.

I met my husband when I was a teenager, and we've been together ever since. He's been by my side throughout all of my achievements over the past nearly twenty years, which is something I just love. We've passed the test of time and continue to grow together more every day.

Even though there were positives to growing up in the country where everyone knows everyone, it also bought with it a culture that can be somewhat limiting. It was difficult to have dreams and think outside of the square, because it was quickly squashed as unachievable and unreachable by some, especially when those dreams were different from the majority. With most people being so conservative, it was hard to be a woman and dream of success, especially in business. It was generally frowned upon, because running a business was a man's job.

However, I knew one day I would find out what the universe had in store for me. I always knew I would be destined for something big, but I didn't know what that would look like for me. As I made my way through the schooling system, I soon realised my destiny was not to be found in formal education. All I knew was that I didn't want to go to university like my friends did.

How did you get into network marketing?

Like a lot of people, I'd never really known what I wanted to do with my life, and it wasn't until the day I was offered a sneak peek into the world of network marketing that I realised I'd finally found what I'd been looking for. I've always had the spirit to help, encourage, and motivate others. I see that now as the entrepreneurial spirit inside of me. Never did I expect my destiny to be wrapped up in this opportunity, especially considering it was in health and wellness, an area in which I had absolutely no experience.

I think that's a key point in network marketing. When I started over three years ago, it was unknown. You don't just wake up one day and decide to be a network marketer. But so many people aren't fulfilled in their life and just live day to day. For me, it felt like that movie, *Groundhog Day*. Get up, run around, go to work, come home, get dinner ready, run around, and then go to bed and try to get excited about doing the same thing again tomorrow. I didn't realise there was another option. Don't be afraid. It's completely normal to have reservations and feel so far out of your comfort zone, you don't even know where to begin.

The best thing about this industry is that it's earn as you learn. What I lacked in experience I made up for with my relentless passion to motivate, support, and inspire others. I had the desire to help people believe they could do whatever they wanted if they put their mind to it and paid no attention to where they lived or their background.

In a traditional workplace, there's so much nepotism and bias. It's not what you know but who you know. The more you do, the more people generally expect. What drew me to this opportunity is that everyone starts at the same spot. It's an effort-based business. No one can jump the work and go straight to the top regardless of who they know or what letters are behind their name. You don't work for someone else's bonuses or promotions. I discovered a whole new lease on my own life when I started my network marketing business. Life had truly begun.

Before starting my network marketing business, I worked fulltime for the Australian Federal Government. I also ran a business with my husband, coached two local netball teams, played netball, and devoted myself to my little girl, Izabella. My life was full, except there were two significant problems with this crazy schedule of working seventy-plus hours a week.

The first, and most significant, was that I often couldn't be with Izabella when it mattered. The hardest moments came when I took her to school and couldn't stay for assemblies like the other mums. It broke my heart to see her disappointed little face. I knew I had to find another way that would enable me to always be there for Izabella.

The second problem was flexibility. Being in the traditional nine-to-five environment didn't give me the chance to have flexibility and control, which everyone wants.

Then, in one day, or actually one phone call, my whole life changed forever. My long-time friend, Chelsea Launer, asked me to take a look at a network marketing business. I will be forever grateful to Chelsea, because without her courage to offer me this business opportunity, my life would be so different today.

At first I was sceptical. I knew I was happy to have a look at the opportunity, as I was actively looking for one that would provide me with greater flexibility and an income that would enable me to get my life back. I was a major financial contributor to my household. I couldn't just leave my job. I had to find something that could potentially replace the fulltime income I was earning at the time.

Once I observed the business presentation, I was automatically hooked. I thought, *Wow this is exactly what I've been asking the universe for.* I was totally surprised to be drawn into the world of health and wellness. To be honest, this did scare me a little. But then I looked at the people who were successful and saw they were just normal people who worked hard, I figured I could do it, too! That's when I made the smartest decision of my life and jumped in, one-hundred percent.

How has having a network marketing business changed your life?

Within seven months I was a Vice President with my company and had created the opportunity to replace my fulltime income. I continued to keep my hectic schedule before resigning from my government job just twelve months after starting my network marketing business. I finally had the freedom to attend Izabella's school assemblies, and I was even able to help out in the classroom. Also, in one of my happiest moments, my husband was able to resign from a job he wasn't happy with but held onto for twenty years to support us. Now he gets to enjoy his work. This opportunity has completely transformed both his life and mine.

After being in the industry and running my business for just over three years, I hit the top of our management structure, where the average income in Australia at that level is just over $24,000 a month. People work their whole lives and never have the opportunity to get to the top of a company.

The top economists are predicting a growth of six-hundred percent in network marketing. It's not a matter of *if* but *when*. This will become the next trillion-dollar industry, with the next wave of millionaires predicted to come out of network marketing companies, specifically in health and wellness.

It's the scariest decision I've ever made, but I'm so grateful to have jumped into it. I'm now creating a legacy for my family, and my daughter's family, that will impact them for generations to come. In this network marketing company, your business is willable, so I can pass this income on to my family forever.

I have a genuine passion to show other people, especially women, how they can also have it all and not rely on others for financial freedom. I'm able to show them they have a choice to put their passion first and make life-changing money at the same time. I'm honoured to help, coach, and train these women. This is the industry that will make it come true, with six out of ten women who earn over $100,000 a year coming from the network marketing/direct-selling industry. There's a choice, and I'm so thankful I chose network marketing. I now look forward to helping others for the rest of my life. I love what I do, so it doesn't feel like work. I get to take time off when I want and travel the world, because my business is run on-line, and on-line businesses are the wave of the future.

I continue to live in my small, rural city and give my daughter the country upbringing my husband and I always envisioned for her, close to her grandparents and family. I also have the means to take her travelling all over the world, so she can see and experience different cultures.

We also have the ability to move to the city and explore bigger and better opportunities. This is all possible, because I stepped out of my comfort zone and believed in myself and what was possible. I also believed I deserved more, and so did my family. It's possible to do whatever it is you desire to in life if you work hard enough and don't give up.

Think about it. You can create a residual income that's not dependent upon you. If you're no longer around, your business keeps running. That's the secret of network marketing. Creating a duplicate business that isn't dependent upon you. And you don't trade time for money. You can do it all and get paid amazingly well. You have so many choices. You just have to know where to look.

Who has inspired and influenced you, and why?

I've had so many people in my life who've been impactful, but here are a few of the biggest inspirations and influences I've had to date.

My husband Brent

Brent inspires me every day to be the best version of myself. The belief he has in me is truly remarkable, and he's always been my biggest supporter in anything I've done. He's the most loving, caring, and supportive man I've ever met and the best father to our beautiful daughter, Izabella.

One of the key factors to success in this business is having a supportive partner, and I couldn't have done any of what I have without his commitment to our goal as a family. He's a role model to other partners in the way support makes a massive difference to success, and how this is a family business and a family commitment. So I want to thank him for showing others how to be the best HNVP EVER, and member of the Behind the Scenes club, as they call themselves. Thanks for doing life with me, Brent. I'm grateful every day you picked me.

My daughter, Izabella

Izabella is the most amazing little girl. She drives me to be a better person and to work hard because of the legacy I want to create for her. She's so kind, just like her dad. She's the most fabulous girl and the next generation of fierce and fabulous women. I never really knew what love was until the day I became her mother, and she's been my biggest and best accomplishment.

My parents

My mum has influenced my life in so many ways. Mostly she's shown me what it means to have a hundred percent support and loyalty from someone. She's always supported me in everything I've done and made me believe I can do whatever I want if I put my mind to it. She's my best friend, and I hope to be half as good of a mother to Izabella as she's been to me. Without her support and help with my family, none of this would be possible. She's always had my back and was there for Izabella when sometimes I wasn't able to.

My dad is the most brilliant mind I've ever met. He's inspired me to be the best I can be. I've watched him achieve so much in his life, and he's always taught me I can do whatever I want, as long as I'm prepared to work hard for it. I thank my dad for my work ethic and my tenacity, traits I've learnt from him. These qualities have helped me to become as successful as I am. He's always been hard on me, teaching me to aspire for greatness and never settle. He's taught me how to create a business and what it takes to make it work. I want to thank him for never giving up on his dreams to allow me to live mine.

My Sister

Sammi was my first friend and has taught me so much. She constantly inspires me. I've watched her grow into an amazing wife and mother. She makes me proud every day. I want to thank her for my beautiful nieces, Harmoni and Ellie. I'm so grateful to her for bringing them into my world. She's always encouraged me. She inspires me to be the best and is living proof you can do whatever you put your mind to.

I want to thank her for the laughs and the fights. It's been amazing to have someone who, no matter what, loves me unconditionally. I'm so excited for our future now that she's joined my network marketing business, because her future is so bright. She inspires me to be a great mother like she is, and I love that our kids get to grow up together. I'm proud of who she's become and that she's now found the love of her life, Con, to complete her family with her stepson, Alex. I look forward to new additions, soon.

My Nan

Nan has given me so much in my life, but mainly she's taught me how to live with strength and resilience. Her strength has been life-changing to me. Her love for our whole extended family has been so inspiring.

Pa showed me what I should expect in a man, with his love for her. He also taught me to be respectful and to work hard. He was a devoted father and Pa, and I miss his lessons in life every day.

I want to thank my Nan for the long chats and the advice. Also, the best apple slice recipe ever. I look forward to sharing so much more with her, and I will be forever grateful for her relationship with Izabella. The love we have for her is unconditional.

Family

My aunties, uncles, and cousins. I've learnt so much from every one of them. Especially my Uncle Dougie, who we've recently lost. I want to thank him for teaching me to stand up for myself, to never let anyone put me down, and to be proud of who I am. This skill has seen me well in my life so far. We miss him so much.

My Aunty Elaine inspired me to live life and be happy. She was always so cheerful and such a blessing to this world. She was taken far too early.

Friends

I've had many friends over the years who've helped me through the good and bad times. These women have constantly encouraged me, supported me, and loved me. Time or distance makes no impact on our friendship. Sarah, Fiona, Belinda, Rachael, Shona, and Lisa are so important to me, and I look forward to many more amazing times in the future. Their belief in me has had a big impact on my life.

Nkandu Beltz

I would like to take the opportunity to acknowledge and thank Nkandu Beltz for helping me bring my dream to life with this book. Her belief in me and the network marketing industry is amazing. I'm grateful every day she's in my life, and I can't imagine my life without her in it. She inspires me, and I'm so proud of what she's achieved in this world. She shines her light so bright and won't let anyone dim it. The world is better place because she's in it. I can't thank my gorgeous friend enough.

Uplines

To my amazing uplines, Chelsea Dolby and Debbie Loughnane. They showed me a different way and led me to a better life. Their constant belief in me has been one of the reasons I've never stopped striving to be the best. They've shown me the way, and I'm just a direct duplication of these two amazing women. Without them, our lives would be so different, and I love them both so much.

I want to thank Debbie for the coaching and the time she's given me and my family to help us grow this business together. I can't thank her and her family enough, but especially Tim, for taking us in and loving us unconditionally. Debbie is a true world-class leader, and I was honoured to help her achieve her biggest goal yet, to become the first 4 Wide NVP in Australia. Her honesty with me has shaped me into the leader I am today.

My sisterlines and sidelines.

I love them all. I want to thank them for stepping out of their comfort zone and running a network marketing business. The world is a better place because of them. I appreciate the lessons they've taught me, especially Lisa and Katina, who are like sisters to me. I'm so grateful to network marketing for bringing them, and their families, into our lives.

My Team

My team is made of important people who trusted in me enough to say yes to partnering with me in this life-changing business. I also want to acknowledge the others who've said yes, and to their teams. They're all amazing vision painters, and together we'll change this world, one person at a time. I wake up every day and get to learn from these change makers. I'm so blessed to work with the best people in the world. They all inspire me and have influenced my life so much.

Kristy, Melissa, Andrea, Sammi, Tracey, Chloe, Lucinda, and Nkandu. Look out, world, because these superstars have only just begun.

What are the three main attributes you feel have helped you the most to be successful in the industry?

BELIEF

I've always believed in myself and my ability to do whatever it is I put my mind to. Even though at times I've felt as though everyone was against me, I stayed true to myself, and my self-belief never wavered. This is important, because in times of hardship, and in network marketing there will be many, you need to dig deep and believe when others won't. Never give up, and you will come out the other end where you want to be.

One thing about network marketing is that it does bring out your weaknesses quickly, which is a good thing. Trust me. You're able to find help from people who support you and identify skills you can work on to improve your life and relationships. Our mind is just like our body and requires fuel to survive, so we must feed it regularly through personal development. My constant bible is *The Secret* by Rhonda Byrne. This book changed my life.

With my extensive background in sport, I considered myself a positive person, until I read this book. I didn't realise I was sabotaging my success with my own thoughts. Keeping your mind strong and filled with love, positivity, and learning what fuels your belief, is something we all must do every day to make sure you're living the best life ever.

It can be a confronting exercise taking a look in the mirror and realising everything you've attracted and created. You must be able to get over it and forgive yourself for your past mistakes. Be open and vulnerable to work on improving your skills.

There have been many times I've lost my belief, and that's when I've had to look in the mirror the hardest. To have the conversations with my uplines and self-evaluate. You can have anything you want in life. You just have to create it. What changed was my ability to be coached and find the skills needed to move past that moment and fill my belief cup right back up again.

DETERMINATION AND PERSISTENCE

I was determined to create a better life for my daughter and to show her that you can do whatever you put your mind to. Giving up was not an option. I was fully committed to the network marketing opportunity and was prepared for the backlash I would face.

Every time someone tried to stop me, I fuelled that into proving them wrong. I didn't let others' opinions affect me, because after all, we can't pay our bills with their opinions. I was so determined, and no matter what, was not giving up.

When I first started, I had a conversation with Chelsea and Deb, and told them both I was going to commit to this for twelve months. Quitting was not an option. That made it easier for them, because they knew I wasn't going anywhere, and they had a free rein to coach me to where I needed to go.

I strongly suggest you have a conversation with your upline. Make yourself accountable, and tell them where you're going and what you want to achieve. This will open the way for the most constructive form of coaching and allow them permission to kick your butt if needed.

I remember a conversation I had with Debbie. I was having a bad time in my business and felt stuck. She was so honest with me. She said, "Beck, you're making it all about you. This business is not about you, it's about changing other people's lives, and you have to go out there and get that essence back, because when you try to blame your team, your uplines, your family, and your lack of support, that's just making it all about you." Sometimes we can't see what we're doing, so we have that confronting conversations with our upline in order to let go off our egos and stop making it about ourselves. So we can get back into activity, lead by example and share this amazing business and product with conviction and passion.

You aren't perfect. You won't always get it right, but if you're willing to keep working, you will come out the other side so much stronger.

WORK ETHIC

I was taught by my father what a strong work ethic was. From a young age I was shown that you don't get anything in life the easy way. Life is not a game of Tattslotto. Whatever you want will not be given, so you need to work for it. I'm so thankful for this message, because network marketing is not rocket science. It takes consistent work over a period of time to be successful. I think people believe it's a get rich-quick-scheme, of which it's most definitely not. Anything in life that's worth it is hard to acquire. When you know the facts and have a solid work ethic, you will succeed at anything `you do.

We've all had times when we haven't given our business what it deserves, but the important thing is to realise that this business can change your life forever, and all you have to do is go back out there and work as hard as you can. This business doesn't take forty hours a week. It takes ten-fifteen hours of consistent work for three-five years to set up your financial future for a lifetime.

As Albert Einstein says, the definition of insanity is doing the same thing over and over again and expecting different results. I was asked where I would be in five years if I didn't make any changes, and this hit me like a tonne of bricks. It brought me to tears. I couldn't go another day on that treadmill I was calling life.

So for me, network marketing was not about whether I had the time or work ethic, or whether I could afford to do it. Physically and emotionally, I couldn't afford to not give this a chance. I couldn't be that person who in five years wished I'd given this a go. I had to work hard and see where it took me. That way I would always be giving this life everything I had and wouldn't have any regrets.

What have been the biggest hurdles you've had to overcome to get to where you are, and how did you get over them?

There have been two big hurdles I've overcome in my journey. The first was the opinions of others and developing a thick skin to cope with judgments about what they think network marketing is.

The other major hurdle is the logistics of living in the country and the extra pressure of having to do a lot of driving. Most people at the top of our company live in a major city. It was difficult to be able to grow the business I have, but I was determined to not let the logistics affect me and prove to everyone that if you work hard enough and believe in yourself, you can do anything you want. I always follow my mantra of focusing on what you can do and not what you can't, so even though I lived in the county and travelled a lot, I would make calls and listen to audio books, and I became the most living, walking, talking product of hours of personal development.

The smaller population means most people weren't open to, or had never even heard of, network marketing. Educating people about the industry and showing them what was possible was my way to overcome this hurdle. I was fiercely determined to show everyone who said I couldn't do to it or that network marketing wasn't a real business, that they were wrong and that this was the real deal. Success speaks the loudest. This is why I worked so hard to get to the top of our company and prove to everyone that it does work and how amazing network marketing can be.

Traditional and conservative views of some people from the country, especially the city I live in, were also difficult to overcome. I decided early on in my business that I was not going to let it affect me, and in fact to show people that the world is changing. There's lots of rejection in this industry, and it's one of the main reasons people give up. But from day one I took the emotion out of it and said I wasn't going to worry if someone said no, because I made a promise to myself that every no would get me closer to a yes. A no right now is not a no forever. You have to be the proof. Some people will jump straight in, and some will watch to see if you succeed before they believe it's for them.

So I made the choice to focus on the good we were doing and the amazing changes we were making in people's lives. We're providing mothers with the chance to come home to their babies and for young people to start their own business. We're allowing people to make choices and not to settle for a life they don't want. We give them the choice and opportunity to step outside of their comfort zone and change their lives for the better.

Our team inspires men and women to be the best versions of themselves and live the life of their dreams, no matter what anyone says. There are no opinions that can take that away from us. I made a choice to focus on the positives and the future, and that's how I overcame the hurdles I faced. My *why* was bigger than my excuses, and my exterior is so thick, it could not be affected.

What would you suggest to those who've just started a network marketing business?

I would suggest that anyone who joins network marketing to set a goal and a *why*. This needs to be so big, it won't allow you to give up when you hit tough times, and trust me, you will. Put yourself in a bubble of resilience and be careful who you choose to spend your time with. Rid yourself of the negative people in your life and surround yourself with positive, likeminded people. Those with their own goals they're working towards. Sometimes the most negative people are the ones closest to you. But this is where you have to be resilient. You're a direct representation of the five people you spend the most time with, so pick them wisely.

Challenge yourself to be so strong, you won't be affected by the opinions of others, and shift those opinions into drive and determination to succeed beyond their belief. Use it as fuel to create the dream you've always imagined.

The only way you can ever fail in network marketing is to give up. NEVER GIVE UP.

If you were able to go back and start again, what would you do differently?

I would build my business bigger and faster. I wouldn't be scared and would share this opportunity with everyone I know. This is the best opportunity in the world, and I missed so many when I first started, because I was scared to talk about it. I would not make that mistake again. I would shout from the treetops and show people how this can change their lives, too. I would use my upline's stories and be confident in the business and the opportunity. I would have shared it with so many more people. When someone in your life rings you with an opportunity, take it. When you have the chance to change their life, and you don't do it because you're too scared, you'll regret it.

I've seen people on my "chicken" list show up at an event. This can be such a slap in the face but one of the best lessons in this business. They joined with someone else, because I made a judgment that this wasn't for them. It's such a selfish thing to do. You don't get to chose someone else's future, and I often think about how brave Chelsea was to share this opportunity with me and not just think I wouldn't be interested. She changed my life forever.

Following the system is vital. Annie Steike, one of the gorgeous Regional Vice Presidents in my team, changed my life forever when she introduced me to Eric Worre. He said it doesn't matter what works, the only thing that matters is what is duplicable. That was a pivotal turning point in my network marketing career. THANK YOU, ANNIE! It showed me to have a clear system and make it simple. So when you start, follow the system of your upline, don't overcomplicate, and keep it simple. This will serve you all the way through your whole network marketing career.

When you decided to leave your job of thirteen years to pursue this business fulltime, were you scared? How did you determine this was the right opportunity for your family?

I was so scared and unsure. I looked at the business I'd created around my fulltime job. I also sat down with my husband and asked him to imagine what I could do and how many lives I could change if I had more time to really work on my business. After that, it was really a no-brainer for us. I would get more time with Izabella and more time to work on my business. It's said if you're not living out of your comfort zone, then you aren't living. I'm an overachiever and always like to live on the edge.

I told Brent that if it didn't work out the way we wanted, it was okay, because it would be an experience and a great story. I told myself, *You know what? I have nothing to lose but everything to gain.* Then I walked in and quit and never looked back.

What still inspires you after three years in your business? What's the vision you have for yourself, your business, and your family?

I now know what's possible, and I've seen how many people need the gift of this business. I'm so excited to share it with everyone I meet and help everyone in my team achieve all of their hopes and dreams. My vision is now bigger and brighter than it's ever been to help my whole family become financially free and give back to the community.

I've laid the foundation. I've created a goal for the future, and that is to help the youth of the country communities achieve their goals with a Leadership Academy. With my network marketing business, I will have the means to create this dream. I have so many reasons as to why I'm inspired every day, and one of them is that I want to show my daughter what this business has taught me and give her the guidance to fulfil her dreams. I love teaching her how to achieve her goals without anyone's help. I want to influence the next generation and be a role model, especially to young girls from the country.

I look forward to living a happy and healthy life surrounded by the doers of the world, not the pretenders, and to work together to make the world a better place. Our future is so bright, and the world is a big place. We haven't even scratched the surface with this amazing network marketing opportunity.

I want to spread life and love everywhere I go, surrounded by my family, where we work together on projects to make the world a better place. This is also what inspires me. In this business, we rise by lifting others.

The company I'm a part of also inspires me with the love and admiration they have for the sales field. It's second to none. We're so blessed to have the best head office team in the world, and the most giving and generous company ever. They spoil us so much. We get gifted things for Christmas, our birthdays, Valentine's Day, and Australia Day. My husband also loves this, as he doesn't have to worry about forgetting a present on these special occasions. I'm proud to stand alongside this company and look forward to being a patriot for network marketing, and our company, in the future. I want to send a thank you to the two Mels, the rocks of our head office team. I appreciate everything they do and what they stand for.

What are some of the best rewards this business has given you?

There have been so many rewards. The Mercedes, the Tiffany, the trips to Las Vegas, New York, Port Douglas, Uluru, and Fiji, and of course, the income.

I've also achieved many awards in my time, but the most memorable is being awarded in the top ten consultants globally in our company for growth and consistency in our Parade of Champions. Having that award presented to me in front on 18,000 people in Las Vegas was one of my most memorable achievements. The very nice citrine Tiffany ring I was gifted was a nice bonus of the award as well.

They've all been life-changing. But the biggest gift has been that I'm able to get back my life and time. The same goes for my husband. Spending more time with my daughter, and giving this gift to others, are two of my greatest rewards.

I remember the day I was handed the keys to my brand-new white Mercedes. It was surreal and magical, but it has nothing compared to what it feels like to hand the keys to someone else who's achieved the same goal. To be the visionary for them to change their life and show them how to live a life of their design. Having people say that because of me, their life, and their children's lives, have been changed forever. There are no words or money that can beat that feeling. That's what the essence of this industry is. Showing people how to change their lives. Rising by lifting others to their goals. It's truly life-changing.

What are your top five tips for success in network marketing?

1. WORK HARD.

   Go out and share this with everyone you know. EVERYONE. Be consistent every week, and you will see results. My mantra is "Don't focus on what you can't do, focus on what you can." At times this will mean sacrifice, but it's only for a short time. My team will tell you that there's no QV in TV, which is me saying to be smart about where you're spending your time. Don't sit on Facebook or watch TV, when you could be out there building your own future, instead of watching other people create theirs. We all have the same twenty-four hours. It's what we choose to do with them that matters.

2. DONT GIVE UP.

   The only way you can fail is to give up. This is a business of building wealth, and it won't happen overnight. You have to commit to it for three to five years, but you won't regret it. Too many people think it's a get-rich-quick scheme and give up right before payday, as I like to say. Be true to your goal and to yourself, and you'll never regret it. Lives will be changed in the process, including your own. Ask yourself where you'll be in five years. If you don't like the answer, then get out there and change your future. Network marketing is the vehicle. All you have to do is go out there and drive it.

3. BELIEVE IN YOURSELF.

   Be so focused on your goal, you don't let anything, or anyone, penetrate your resolve to get it. Plug into trainings from your uplines and conferences. Do personal development every day. Surround yourself with likeminded and inspirational people, and this will fill up your belief cup. From the hardest times comes your best success. Just hold your belief, and then get into action. THE LEARNING IS IN THE DOING

4. LISTEN TO YOUR UPLINE, AND BE COACHABLE.

This is vitally important. You need to listen to, and learn from, the people who've gone before you. One of the reasons people don't succeed in network marketing is that they come in and try to reinvent the wheel. Instead, they should spend the time listening to their upline and sharing the product and the business. Any time spent trying to change systems is wasted, because this is a relationship business, and you have to go out there and share this opportunity and business with belief and passion. You have to go and talk to people, as network marketing is a belly-to-belly business.

Be open to constructive criticism to work through any barriers you may have. One of the main reasons I've been successful is because I've given my uplines an open door for feedback. They're able to tell me what I need to know, even if I don't want to hear it, particularly if I'm blocking my own growth. My uplines have been honest, and even though at times I haven't liked it, I've taken their advice on board and changed. My business has grown because of that. Listen and learn. Uplines are the pioneers. Their hindsight can be our foresight. If you listen to your master, Yoda, or in my case, Debbie Loughnane, "Then succeed you will."

5. HAVE FUN.

This is the most important, because if it's not fun, you won't want to keep doing it. Laugh at yourself and know that as humans, we're not perfect. We do the best we can. I laugh so much in this business. Don't take life too seriously. After all, life is about living it to the fullest and having fun. I know every time I step out my front door I'm having fun, and that's why I love what I do. You won't have this much fun making a living anywhere else than you do in a network marketing business. #fact

CHAPTER 3

Amanda Holland

"Our deepest fear is not that we are inadequate. Our deepest fear is that we are powerful beyond measure. It is our light, not our darkness, that most frightens us."

Marianne Williamson

～⌒⌒～

CHAPTER THREE

Amanda Holland

What is your background? What was your childhood like?

I was lucky enough to be raised in a family of six children. We grew up in a beautiful country town living outdoors, climbing trees, and riding bikes down big hills with our legs up on the handlebars and arms up in the air. We were protected from the crazy world out there. My parents were influential in the community and had strong religious beliefs.

I was a creative child and a big dreamer. In my mind I believed I could do anything. When I was eight years old, the Moscow circus came to Australia, and I asked my mum and dad if we could go. Of course, with a family of six kids the answer was no, so I decided I'd just bring the Moscow circus to my backyard. I did a letterbox drop and asked all of the neighbours to come.

The day arrived. I had three chairs set up, and I made some circus- looking things. There was an A4 piece of paper stuck on the carport that read, *Welcome to the Moscow Circus*. No one ever came, but the show went on. I remember forgetting quickly about the guests not being there, and knowing me, I probably didn't put the date or time on the invitation. I look back at these wonderful memories and realize how much beauty there was in experiences like this and how as adults these childhood events can shape us or prevent us from reaching greatness.

I had a lot of love and joy to share and would always dream of the beautiful world I wanted to see. I often felt like the outsider, because I always believed there was something greater than me. My father, a truly wonderful man, said all of the bad things I thought would happen were all made up in my head. I was the dreamer. I was creative. I loved trying new things and loved seeing people happy. I wanted to be a part of it somehow and inspire this happiness, but it was a battle, especially through my teenage years when I was trying to find my place and to simply fit in.

What were some of your early jobs?

At the wonderful age of eighteen I became a mum to a beautiful little boy named Ethan. This was the most wonderful day of my life and where I learnt that I didn't need to fit in anywhere. I just needed to be the best me. The best mum for him. That's where the legacy began.

I got my first job only three months after having Ethan, as I knew I had to take responsibility. I would ask myself often why I should have less because I was eighteen, not married, and had no financial backing. Why could I not create it all? My answer was that I didn't have to be this person society saw me as, and it was up to me to create my life.

It's so crazy to think that society has conditioned us all to stereotype and label almost everything and everyone. In the beginning, being seen as the young, single-mum stereotype in the eyes of society really rattled me.

I remember one day when I was servicing an attractive young woman. She had on a pair of jeans by the latest Australian designer. I told her how much I loved the jeans, and that she looked great in them. She replied with, "Maybe one day you'll be able to afford them".

I was so confused. We'd been having this great conversation. She'd asked about me, and I mentioned I was eighteen and had a beautiful little boy. I also told her what suburb I lived in. As most people did who I came across, she'd already made up her mind about me.

That week I waited for my pay to come in, and it was exactly enough for not one, but two pairs of my favourite jeans. I wondered why I should be any different. I could have the jeans, too. Of course, that means I went without almost everything that week. My petrol even ran out on my way to work. I had to ring my brother to give me ten dollars, which was just enough to get me there and back home, because I'd spent all of my money on the hot jeans I was wearing. It's so funny how words can affect you. I always have to ask myself how I receive them and what to do with them.

This was another defining moment that shaped the future of which road I would take. I could have easily felt sorry for myself and thought I'd never have what others have, or I could go and get it. It had to be up to me.

At the age of twenty I started my own salon business, mostly because I needed to get by and pay my rent and put food on the table. Another part was definitely because I felt, again, that I needed to fit in and show I could do this. I was able to constantly be around people and learn from them, but most importantly, I was able to give back. Sometimes it was through a beauty service to make someone feel amazing, so they would leave with a big smile on their face.

I wouldn't survive if I was just doing a service every hour of the day. I have a great desire, like many in this industry, to love people and allow them to be.

During my ten years being a salon owner, I was blessed with my second son, Oliver, with my partner Saade. I had my family. Life was good. I had a busy salon with two employees and was booked six to ten weeks ahead of time. We had a great income, but we had no lifestyle. I was always working. I had become so conditioned to believe that it was normal to work forty to sixty hours a week.

And when I wasn't working, I was climbing trees, kicking footballs, and constantly asking myself, *Am I a good mum? Have I spent enough time with them?* I was trying to be the best of everything to everyone and make them happy. I was the best partner, daughter, sister, and friend. There was one problem. I wasn't being the best for me. At just twenty seven, I was slowly breaking.

Then along came my best friend, Rachel Mau, who is my ray of sunshine. She introduced me to Network Marketing. Although I couldn't see what was happening to me at the time, as I was in survival mode and on autopilot, I knew my business owned me. My best friend could see I deserved more time to reap the rewards of my hard work and that she could offer me more through this fantastic network marketing company.

As a working mother with two little men in my life and a business that took me away, I welcomed the change, and now I'm the happiest woman and so grateful I was offered this opportunity from Rachel. As she looked through the exterior of the busy salon, she saw the wonderful mum, great partner, best friend, and the happy Mandy who always said she was amazing. She saw me. She saw a woman who truly deserved to not have to say "Maybe one day" anymore. The people in my life deserved so much more.

I will never forget the first conversation between Rachel and me, when I felt myself start dreaming again. I said, "Rach, if I could be where you are in two years, it could change so much." Rachel replied with, "Mandy if you really want to do this, and know that I'm here with you, you'll have it all much sooner than two years.

In that same year we were able to celebrate together driving out of the dealership with our new Mercedes Benzes we were rewarded for reaching management level. I remember looking in my rear-view mirror and seeing Rachel in her beautiful car and thinking that if someone had told me just one year ago we'd both be here right now driving out of this dealership with not just a pretty car, but so much more, I would have thought they were the ones dreaming. Those dreams I had were becoming my reality.

What a beautiful and truly humbling way to become successful. To offer someone an opportunity that could completely change their life. To walk beside them and empower them to have the same kind of success. To have their own business where they decide not only what to do next but how much or how little. Become successful by helping others become just as successful.

How did working all of the time affect your family?

So many people are wrapped up in what needs to get done, that we forget our little ones are watching and learning from us. We're their inspiration. We're all they know, so when we're depleted, we're showing them this is normal. It doesn't matter what we say. They're looking at our actions.

My children played a huge role in my saying a big yes to my network marketing business. Especially my son, Ethan, who was just ten years old when I started. A short eight months later this business not only matched my beauty business income, it doubled it. Ethan saw I was excited and dreaming again. He saw me sometimes doubt my abilities, but he also saw me rise above it and just do it. He saw me achieve.

My younger son, Oliver, was only two at the time. Now at almost five years old, he observes me and his big brother being happy. It's a ripple flow!

Beautiful Ethan and I were on a walk one sunny evening, and he said, "Mumma I have to tell you something. You have shown me that anything is possible and that I can create whatever I want."

What are your three favourite things about Network marketing?

First is the time I have back. Before, I would often wonder about what I'd love to do if I had the time, but then reality would kick in, and my dream would be shattered. It was impossible to leave work for an extended period of time, whether it was to take a course or just do nothing. Who was going to pay me, and what would happen to my business?

So many people know there's more out there for them, but they just can't see how it will ever be possible to pull away from what they're doing and have the financial backing to do so. My network marketing business has allowed me to take as much time as I need. I created a second income stream alongside my existing business that has now become my main income stream.

This is where choice comes in. It goes hand in hand with the feeling of freedom.

Imagine your network marketing business has become your main income stream, and you have your time back. You can take that long holiday you've dreamt about for so long. You can pursue your desires and dreams, whether it's another business or a charity or to just *be*. Now imagine being paid for this. It's the vehicle to drive you to what's next.

It has absolutely brought me back to trusting that my future will be amazing. I now have time and financial freedom, and it has given me so many choices as to how I spend my days.

What have been the biggest hurdles you've had to overcome to get to where you are, and how did you get over them?

I truly believe that when working with people you learn so much about yourself. That's the true lesson in life. I've found that with this business. I've learnt I truly deserve to be fulfilled and happy and step into what I know I can create. This was one of the hardest concepts for me to grasp during my youth. The guilt of society constantly putting pressure on me.

You're not home enough

Is this really possible?

Why would you need to do this if you were happy?

Are you looking after yourself?

Put yourself first.

You're working too much.

We never see you.

I was unable to say no to customers, as I was grateful to have such a booming business, and it fulfilled our financial desires. Everything I felt guilty about was impossible for me to change while I owned the salon.

It felt impossible to ever feel set free from the limiting thoughts regarding my present and my future. I have absolutely learnt that I was just one decision away from complete change, and sometimes this can be the biggest hurdle to get over. Get out of your own way and make the change.

 I'm so glad I did.

How did you manage to implement your network marketing business into your life when you were running a busy beauty salon?

I believed so much that I could do this, and I had to have results quickly. I had a great desire to have everyone who was supporting my vision, looking at joining me, or had already joined me, to make my goals a reality. It's the same as when I was eighteen. Why shouldn't I have all of the things we've been conditioned to think we can't have? I had to take on the responsibility and create it,

So at the time I was working at the salon, my crazy life consisted of forty to sixty-hour weeks. Some nights I didn't get home until ten p.m., and often had to get up at five a.m. on Saturdays. I accepted that life was happening around me whether I liked it or not. It was something I couldn't control, but I could control how big or small I saw this opportunity.

In the early days, when I first started the business, I did say to myself, *Short-term sacrifice for the long-term gain.* I figured I could really give this a red-hot go, or I could spend the next thirty years watching life pass me by. For my kids to grow up and be that person who talks about everything they're going to do *one day* or wonder about all of the things they wished they'd done. This scared the living daylights out of me. It's crazy to think that I thought it was normal to believe when I retired, that I could live and travel. My reality now is that I don't know what tomorrow will bring, so why would I not do it now? There was no way I was going spend another minute wasting my time.

Still today. I consistently grow and coach my beautiful team on VISION! I tell them to get it crystal clear, and the rest will follow. I had to really commit myself to spend the small amount of time I had productively. Not sitting behind a computer or talking about everything I wanted to do. I got in front of people, told them about my vision, and let them know that anyone who would love to come with me and had the same commitment, we could go there together. How awesome is that?

Communication with my support was key. My children, partner, and friends kept me constantly accountable to my words. I knew to maintain their belief in me, and especially for my two boys, I had to show them my commitment to what I said and to not give up on my dream. It's always *we* and not *I* in my communication with family, and keeping them involved with what *we* as a family are creating together. My vision and *knowing* was greater than my reality at the time. Just like the Moscow Circus in my backyard, the show still had to go on, even though no one came. It took my one-hundred percent commitment to my words and a *no-matter-what* attitude.

Who has inspired and influenced you, and why?

The memory of my dad's and mum's constant belief in me, my family, and my team, but mostly my children. THEY WATCH EVERYTHING. *Monkey see, monkey do.*

My parents being the influential people they were, and their great belief and faith in their own religion, has taught me so much as an adult. So many times as a child I found it hard to understand their belief and commitments, but as a thirty year old and as a mother myself, I believe they're the evidence that when you have an unwavering belief in something, and you have trust in the process, then many awesome and wonderful miracles will happen. They were my example. Life threw them some hardship, like when the critics and negative people pulled them down or when it was all just too hard, and they never made the decision to let it knock them down. They never ever gave up on their faith. My parents were truly selfless people, and I believe they had everything their hearts desired, because they shared what they had in order to see others rise, while they rose with them.

I've come to learn that not all of us have the support we feel we require to go out and build on our dreams, and we can all sit in the excuse of "I don't get support from anyone, and I have no one to help me," but that won't get you where you want to go.

I love that in this business, you can start with nothing, and all you need is the support of the person who offered you this opportunity by your side, teaching you and believing in you. It's taking responsibility to make a decision and trust that you know you can create a support network through meeting positive and amazing people that are on the same page. How refreshing is that?

Rachel Mau, who was so brave in sharing this opportunity with me and my family and contributed greatly in believing in the life she knew I deserved. She absolutely inspired me by giving me the evidence of what's possible, so I knew I could do the same. She didn't just change my path, but the ripple flow has been incredible. The time I now have with my family, the time I sit present with my children, the generational change that will now be passed on to Ethan and Oliver to work to live, not live to work. I thank her for what she's given me and for everything else yet to come.

My Uplines, Rachel Mau, Emily Loughnane, and Debbie Loughnane. Without their unwavering commitment to what they all do, and their belief and mentoring they openly share with all of us, we couldn't have achieved all we have.

My amazing team. The best team ever! My best friends and family. I thank them from the bottom of my heart for dreaming and believing in my vision. Most importantly for taking that vision and owning it, growing it, and making it their own reality. I thank them for their belief in me, as I'm still like that young girl who just wants everyone to be happy. Because of their belief, my belief is unwavering.

Nkandu and Bec for giving me the honour to be a part of this book to inspire all of you reading right now to make YOUR change.

Ethan and Oliver for always seeing me. They're the best two little boys in my life. Ethan always reminds me that I can do this. He believes in me to inspire him and Ollie to always believe in themselves. He's the best big brother to Oliver and the best role model and best friend to him.

Saade, who constantly reminds me I can do this.

Mum, Craig, Leanne, Fiona, Dale, and Kerrie for being the most supportive mum and brothers and sisters ever for whatever I chose in life. They're always there for me, no matter what. I'm forever grateful every day for them

How do you stay motivated in your business, and how do you motivate others to stay motivated?

I can't motivate anyone, but I can inspire them. This takes me finding my own motivation to inspire others to do the same.

I always use the example of a client and a personal trainer. When summer approaches, the thought of getting into bathers or something a little more exposing, frightens the daylights out of us. So we find the *motivation* within ourselves to pick up the phone and ring our local personal trainer.

But the trainer can't come to your house to get you out of bed and get you through that door for the dreaded first few sessions. You have to find the motivation to get out of bed and decide you're going to put on your gym gear, get down there, and say "I'm ready! I'm scared, but I'm doing this, and I'm committed."

The trainer can then inspire you through your commitment, motivation, and trust in them and the vision of what's possible.

I really believe to find my own motivation comes from a passion, and if I don't have one, then I find one, and the motivation comes naturally

Exercise, healthy eating, personal development, and a healthy balance of time between family, friends, and business. Have a goal and always move towards it. Don't look in the rear-view mirror, and keep your eyes on the road ahead. Being the evidence of what you coach and share is the absolute key. Recognise your achievements and growth, but also face the hard times head on. Don't ignore your problems, as they will just creep up elsewhere along the way. Face it, talk about it, and accept that it's yours. Stop reliving the past, take responsibility for the way you react to it, and move forward.

If you were able to go back and start again what would you do differently?

Nothing. It was a big yes for me. I had no idea what I was doing, and I didn't know what network marketing was, but I did know how many people were looking for change.

What have been some of the rewards and recognitions you have achieved in your network marketing business?

Reaching Regional Vice President in eight months, earning five-star holidays with my family, and walking the stage in Vegas in front of thousands to be recognised as number sixteen globally. This last one is funny, as I had no idea what I was being recognised for and had to ask some of the others backstage who were also being recognised. I felt terrible at the time that I didn't know, but now I think it's really special.

It's like I knew what this could do not only for me, but for so many others as well. By helping them achieve and inspiring them through my own vision, it planted a seed into their vision. I believe it's not about having to know everything about what you're doing. It's knowing where you're going and committing to it, so whoever partners with you will come with you. This is what the recognition is all about. Promoting out a great amount of managers that are now leading the way for their own teams with their own vision.

I think all of my recognition has been a surprise to me, as I never really think about what I can gain. But I know what this can absolutely do for others, and I have a great need and urgency to commit to showing them the amazing possibilities of what I'm living. What a great way to then be recognised, through seeing your team achieve and hold their achievement proudly. To see them also become just as successful. That's how we become successful. TOGETHER!

What is your advice to someone who owns a beauty salon and is sceptical of this industry?

I truly believe that working in a salon, you're in the most ideal place to say yes to network marketing.

It would have to be one of the most rewarding ways to sell a product. If you're currently in the industry, you may know that service alone versus the overhead and costs to run a business is just not enough. There's a lot of pressure, especially put on employees, to up-sell products. I have never been the type who loves the up-sell or the upset. What I do love about my network marketing business is that when you have an opportunity like mine in the palm of your hands, and you know you have the best product and have built the relationships, friendships, and trust with your clients, then they will naturally ask you what you're so happy about. If they want to know what you're wearing, they will simply ask you.

People are always watching what you're doing, and if you're interesting enough, they will ask you what your secret is. The customer wants to feel great and will ask you, the professional, what they can do to achieve it. A product can lead to a business opportunity, and the business opportunity will lead to the product.

Can I inspire you by saying I've met most of my network marketing team through my shop? It's not because I asked everyone to take a look, but when they see the evidence of what my second business allowed me to do and gave back to me, they asked questions. Be the evidence and know where you're going. Many will follow. Warren Buffet said, "Say yes, learn the rest later."

Can you take a holiday every quarter? Can you book a holiday over the Christmas period? Do you have the choice of evenings at home with family or out with friends? For me to have a Saturday off for the first time in many years was crazy.

When I worked at the salon, there were many times I would cry when my kids were sick, and I would lay in bed thinking about how I could possibly get through the next day. The kids either had to go to school or come to work with me, when they just wanted a cuddle at home and to stay in their pyjamas and get better.

I now don't have to worry about our life fitting in around my business. My network marketing business fits around my family.

The salon owns you. This is totally the wrong way around. If you want it to, network marketing will absolutely change that and get you to own your own time.

What does your future look like now, because of this network marketing opportunity?

My future as a thirty year old looks pretty different to a lot of other Gen Y around me. In fact, it looks different from most people I know. I love this, as it's not just for me. It can be for everybody, and I'm the evidence alongside thousands of others who have created the same kind of life.

I have created the *freedom*. It's my new favourite word!

Freedom of time

Freedom of choice

Freedom of financial burdens

So as a salon owner, my salon owned me and my time. Through my saying YES to network marketing, I officially don't work at my shop anymore. When I do work there, it's by choice to help out the girls or just to hang out with my beautiful clients. I don't have the stress of what to do next and wondering how I'm going to do it. Instead, its now, "I'm doing it"

The simple things like going to the beach with a girlfriend on my own and not going through the guilts, because I've been at work all week and haven't seen my family. I get to see my family so much, that I feel guilty not seeing my friends.

The future is quite different not only for me, but for my children. It blows me away how we pass the baton down to our children and through the generations.

What are your tips for Gen Y to succeed in network marketing?

- We haven't lived enough to know some of what life can throw us. Jump in and be excited, energetic, and fresh. We have our lives at our doorstep, and by golly, how brilliant is that?

- We truly have a blank page where we can write our future the way we want, not the way we're told.

- It's comes down to that beautiful word, *choice*. When I say to myself, *It's my choice*, I feel like I can breathe.

"We rise by lifting others."

Robert Ingersoll

CHAPTER 4

Annie Steicke

Chapter Four

Annie Steicke

What is your background?

Picture this. It's a beautiful, crisp morning, the sun is shining, and there isn't a sound in the schoolyard. It's seven a.m., and I'm in the office madly preparing work for my students. With so much to do, I'm already disappointed in myself, as I wanted to be at school at 6:30. This disappointment with myself was a regular occurrence.

Before I started my network marketing business, I was a teacher at a secondary school who took on more responsibilities than I could often handle. I always thought there was something missing in my professional career, so I put my hand up to see if I could fill that gap. I worked in student wellbeing, student management, transition and pathways, and sports leader. As I began my business, I moved away from the traditional school setting and worked for the education department, where I took part in establishing alternative learning settings for vulnerable youth within the Northern Mallee.

Due to that feeling of a missing piece in my life, my going the extra mile meant I put in *copious* amounts of overtime and went to bed most nights with my laptop trying to catch up with the dream of getting in front. I took work home with me every night, so that meant I had no home time or a moment to relax. And if I did relax, I would often feel guilty I wasn't completing school work. My work-life balance was heavily skewed, and I often wished for a job that would allow me to leave work at work.

Recognition for this extra effort was scarce. While at school and doing extra duties, I had what I could only describe as a sinking feeling, and some busy days I would fly by the seat of my pants. This, again, made me feel guilty, as I always wanted what was best for the students and didn't want to let them down. Then there was the awful feeling of *Sunday-itis*. My Sunday was packed with school preparation. It was draining, and I hated this feeling. I love to be organised and succeed at everything I put my hand up for, so that feeling of disappointment was back again.

Don't get me wrong, there are aspects of teaching I absolutely loved. As I write honestly about my worries with the profession, I want to be clear that teaching has provided me with so many positives. The relationships with the students, parents, and colleagues are priceless. Encouraging students to strive and believe in their dreams was something I valued. However, as I reflect, I realise I never afforded the same courtesy to myself.

How did you get into network marketing?

During the summer holidays of 2013, I received a call out of the blue from a stranger claiming to have acquired my number off an old friend and explained she had a business opportunity. I'll be honest. The call wasn't great. I was rude and dismissive, but due to my nature of "Can't say no," in the bid to finish the call I agreed to view the information about the business and trial the products.

It's amazing how an *out-of- the-blue* moment can be one of the most significant in your life. I'm grateful for that call every day.

Let's move away from the rainbows and unicorns for a moment, as I need to tell you I didn't jump into the business immediately. I watched the information twice, trialled the products for a week, and after numerous phone conversations and providing every objection possible, one night I dreamt of the Network Marketing Company and knew I was in. So I took a deep gulp and said yes! I will never forget my husband's response when I told him about what I'd started. Simply, yet wonderfully, he stated "Well, you'd better just make it work then, Annie," and that's exactly what I did. I'm so thankful for my husband, Kyle, that he backed me from the beginning, as I couldn't run this business without him. I'm a dreamer, and Kyle is the logical, sensible one. It takes a lot for him to understand my massive vision and dream, but I work hard to make him proud every day.

The random stranger, Rebecca McIntyre, and my old friend, Kristy Davidson, are now two important people to me, and I can't imagine life without them. I'm so lucky to work with this calibre of people. The words *thank you* just don't cut it when it comes to wanting to show my appreciation.

My network marketing business has provided my life with so much more than financial freedom. Sure, that was a large factor in the beginning, but the relationships formed and having these people in my life as dear friends, is an immeasurable gift. I put my life events in my calendar first, and then my business activity. My work fits around my life and not the other way around.

I've realized that everything I loved about teaching, what I felt was missing, is being fulfilled with my network marketing business. I'm still teaching, coaching, and empowering people to dream big. The beauty of being able to gift people with this opportunity and an ability to see the greatness in themselves is a privilege. In how many jobs can you say you've changed lives whilst living the life you design?

What are your three favourite things about Network Marketing?

1. LIFE BY DESIGN.

    How often do you get an opportunity to build a business that's based around you and your life? Most people in my life previous to network marketing hated aspects of their job. It's true what they say about finding something you love and you'll never work a day in your life.

    When I was a little girl, I had no idea that something would be network marketing. I was born to be a part of this business, and I hope you find that thing that excites and motivates you. That gives you an overwhelming feeling of joy knowing you're in the right place and that you've found your purpose. I love the quote from Mark Twain. It's on my dream board. He says, "The two most important days in your life are the day you are born and the day you find out why."

2. IT'S EFFORT-BASED

    There's something in network marketing for everyone. Being an effort-based business means you get out what you put in. Some people, like myself, love striving for the top level of leadership and incredible rewards, while others are happy with receiving what they need. In the teaching profession, you were rewarded financially for how many years you'd been in the profession and not how much effort you put in or the success you had. I once had a conversation with a fellow teacher about how we could have put in triple the hours of preparation compared to the teacher across the corridor, but the system wouldn't recognise that.

3.   RECOGNITION, RELATIONSHIPS, REWARD, AND GRATITUDE.

The saying goes that people work harder for praises then they do for raises. This is a signature trait of my personality type. I thrive on recognition and strive for it in everything I do. I hope you don't read this and think I sneeze and look for my name to be up in lights and a round of applause. I just believe that you should never take anything for granted, and showing and receiving gratitude is life-changing. Being rewarded and thanked for improving lives is addictive, and the more you help others achieve their dreams, the more you'll achieve yours.

What have been the biggest hurdles you've had to overcome to get to where you are, and how did you overcome them?

When speaking about being born to be a part of network marketing, I certainly don't mean I haven't had my fair share of obstacles and time out of my comfort zone. What I wish I had known from the beginning of my business was that in order to sustain consistent success, I had to build my skills, and that there were specific skills for network marketing.

I paid respect to the teaching profession. I went to university for four years, and every year whilst teaching I participated in large amounts of professional development. When it came to network marketing, I didn't show it the respect is required and didn't initially learn the skills needed to be productive. The absence of this specific skill set meant my business lacked consistency and would peak and trough like a heartbeat.

My team members and I would be riding high in our businesses and then would hit a common hurdle in network marketing, but we wouldn't know it was perfectly normal or how to deal with it, and our business would suffer. Many decided network marketing doesn't work and walked away instead of learning and improving. It was amazing that when I learnt these skills and taught others in the team, our businesses transformed.

There are key skills needed in the network marketing profession as a collective, and I learnt every one of them from Eric Worre. Of course, I've learnt from my sponsors and sisterlines, however Eric Worre's teachings were a real *light bulb* moment.

This business is about finding, inviting, and following up with potential business partners or clients, doing it right, and promoting events. To make people feel special and to dream. Learn how to do these correctly, and your business will thrive.

You started your network marketing business before you had your daughter, Millie. Was there a benefit to doing that? And what advice do you have for people who think this is something they might do when they have children?

Because of my network marketing business, as a new mother I now have the luxury of choice. The choice to stay at home and raise my daughter. The choice of purchasing the best for her, and the choice to build my business around her needs. I've seen many mothers have no choice but to return to work, and as I grew personally, building the business went from having extra money coming in for luxury items, to building a business and income, especially with future children in mind.

Since becoming a mum, I don't have to go back to the traditional work setting if I don't want to. I have the choice. What a powerful gift to give a mother. The choice to stay at home and enjoy every milestone, a choice to go back to the workplace for a day if you want to, not because you have to, the choice of what pram you want regardless of price, the choice to be happy and comfortable to live life without a super-tight budget. My mission now is to help as many mothers as possible to live the same reality, and I know that's a goal for many of us in the industry.

How do you stay motivated in your business, since you live in the country and have to travel a lot to the cities to attend events and trainings?

Technology has allowed me to remain plugged in, despite the distance. I also get in the car and go to as many events as I can, including our Global Training Conference in Las Vegas. Is it easy and convenient? Absolutely not.

Is it worth it and vital for belief, education, and a sense of belonging in my business? One-hundred percent yes! There have been personal sacrifices for the decision to make the effort to stay connected, and I've had to become super flexible around my family, but I see it as short-term pain for long-term gain. I'm giving up a little now to have a future where I don't have to miss a single thing. Like picking up my children from school. I learnt early on that an event always needs you. When you're up in the business, the event needs your energy and presence, and when you're flat, you need the event to fill your cup again.

Mindset is the most important factor when dealing with living in the country or at a distance from events and trainings. Turn what some people may see as a barrier into an opportunity. I make use of that travel time to listen to audio books and to complete coaching calls with my business partners, as well as making client calls using my car's Bluetooth. It's a chance to make use of that time rather than wasting it by listening to the radio. One of my favourite quotes comes from Zig Ziglar: "People often say that motivation doesn't last. Well, neither does bathing – that's why we recommend it daily."

Every day I listen to an audio or read information that motivates me. It's a life-changing habit.

If you were able to go back and start again, what would you do differently?

In the beginning I approached my business with excitement, love, and "If you need me, I'm there!" I didn't have an easy-to-follow set of steps to begin this business, and I felt it was up to me. It was my responsibility to ensure everyone was successful. After all, people trusted me to begin a network marketing business, so if they didn't succeed, I must be a poor business partner. This was a hard, yet important, lesson to learn, as being everything to everyone simply doesn't work in network marketing. A quote that resonated with me since starting my business is from the wonderful Eric Worre: "It doesn't matter what works, it matters what duplicates."

In turn, I needed to create a business that was self-sufficient and not reliant upon me. We're a team of independent consultants, however I wasn't empowering my team to be independent, and everyone suffered. This swift change actually ended up being a blessing in disguise. It forced me to go back to step one and think, *If I was to start again, how would I do this differently?*

First, I wouldn't be shy about offering people this opportunity. I originally hid that I was a part of network marketing. I had such big aspirations, and I wasn't sure if this was anything more than some little lipstick business. I had the voice of doubt in my head saying:

"No one can even pronounce your company's name."

"How on earth can you sell skincare with acne scars?"

"You went to university, and now you're selling health and wellness?"

"What will my family and friends think?"

Everyone has doubts when starting a new chapter in life but you'll notice every doubt I listed is focused around me. Starting out I worried about myself too often. When I shifted my goals and focused on contribution to others, my business and life improved. What I know for sure is that you need to be passionate about helping others, and that's where success lies. As time continued on, I could see this was an amazing opportunity that could change my family's life forever but also so many others lives as well.

What do you believe is the main reason you've succeeded in this industry while others haven't?

I want to assure you as you're reading this, to please understand I'm no different from you. I wouldn't class myself as someone who was raised with a silver spoon, and that's why I'm where I am today. Please know my upbringing was wonderful. I come from a large family who live in a small country town and all have a great work ethic.

The reason why I've succeeded in this industry, and why you can, too, is that I understand success is the sum of small efforts repeated day in and day out. Don't place success on an unachievable pedestal. Do the steps and activity that matter in your business, do them well, and do them consistently, and success will come in the form of recognition.

It's interesting how people only see your business highlight reel. They don't understand that obtaining success and recognition doesn't always involve glamorous tasks. You need to be tenacious with your goals. Never give up, and no matter what, always have an unwavering belief that you're on the right path. Listen to those who've walked the journey before you. Their wisdom is priceless.

Whilst working on my skills in the industry, I learnt there will be two situations where people will comment to you about network marketing. I've experienced both. In the beginning people will think you're crazy for giving this a go and working hard. Once you're successful, people will call you lucky! There isn't an in-between or another level. In saying this, there are some tips I think will help you with your success.

1. Lead by example

Be the best at what you do and inspire others. If you're rocking your business and in constant activity, then guess what? So is your team. That simply becomes normal to them. When amazing effort every month becomes standard, imagine the possibilities of pushing your business that one step further and where it could take you.

2. Listen, watch, practice, and be a sponge.

I really want to emphasise that we all didn't wake up one morning and know everything about our businesses. We earnt while we learnt, as this process serves as a massive blessing when helping others. Learning how to deal with problems and becoming solution-orientated due to experience, helps to support your business partners. Leave your ego at the door and learn as much as you can from those who've blazed the trail. As the saying goes, "You don't have to be great to start, but you need to start to be great." So get going and chase your dreams. Life isn't a dress rehearsal, so stop playing small.

3. Be clear with your goals.

Achieving them should have a ripple effect of helping others. Know what the first month, six months, and year in your business is going to look like. Don't focus so much on the nitty gritty of the *how* you will achieve it. Just know what you want. Use smart, simple resources and plan. Without preparation and guidance, the excitement of your new business and business partners can fizzle out into, "I don't know what I should do," followed by no activity and people putting it into the too-hard basket and walking away.

Be there to empower new business partners to achieve their targets and demonstrate how to run a successful business. Build confidence and self-worth. It's the best thing you can do, and the reward is immeasurable.

Who has inspired and influenced you, and why?

My mother has been the biggest influence in my life. I don't want to discount my father in my life influences. Dad has shown me what a hardworking father does for his family. He worked so hard to provide for us, and I know my siblings and I appreciate that.

As the only girl with four older brothers, I feel my mother's character and achievements inspired this young girl to dream big. Her story is a great one. At eighteen years of age, she was the first child in her family to go away to study. She attended Sacred Heart Teachers College and lived on residence there.

You could say that Mum had it pretty tough when away studying to become a teacher. She didn't have a car, so she often walked to get places. When she could afford it, she would sneak out of lectures early on Friday to catch the train home to see her family. She was paid thirty dollars a fortnight on a studentship, yet had to pay twenty dollars for board. She did that for two years.

After teaching for four years at a Catholic primary school, she was invited to be Principal. She was the first female lay Principal at the school. She held that position for three years before having to resign to start a family.

After being away from teaching for twenty-seven years to raise a family, due to my brother and I wanting to go to university to further our study, Mum applied and was appointed as principal of the local Catholic primary school. With children at home, Mum went back to university to update her qualifications. This meant having to travel to regular weekend lectures, as well as working fulltime and looking after a household. Talk about leading by example and getting it done, Mum!

She was principal of the Catholic primary school for fifteen years, with her greatest achievement being the improvement of buildings and resources, through grants for children in a rural setting. Improving the lives of others via resources and opportunity… sound familiar?

My mum didn't realise it at the time, but her ambition and aspirations made her an amazing role model for her only daughter. She taught me that if you work hard, you can do it all and do it well. When I reflect on her decision to return to the workforce, I know she did that so my brother and I didn't have to struggle through university like she did. It breaks my heart when I reflect on the many SOS calls I made to her asking for more money, as she wouldn't have had the same comfort. Now I have my parents on my dream board, as the more I build my network marketing business, the more opportunity I have to be able to provide for them when they're older. A gift and ability I wouldn't be able to afford if I was still teaching.

My parents always provided us with what they could, but with such a large family, Christmas and birthdays didn't always involve expensive gifts. But we never missed out. It's funny how as a young child I counted my blessings through material gains and compared my belongings to my peers. Now that I'm older. I feel so lucky to have all of my brothers in my life. The relationships are priceless and way better than fancy gifts.

My business partners are huge influences in my life. Every person in our team mean the world to me. It's hard to think about life without these amazing people. I wouldn't have ever known some of my closest friends if it wasn't for them being introduced into network marketing. My business has brought me back to dear childhood friends. How can you put a price tag on that sort of fulfilment?

Nurturing relationships and making a positive impact in another's life is a privilege. That's what enticed me to pursue teaching. Something I've learnt, and hope you will, too, is to always strive to better yourself for your team. They say your business will only grow to be as big as you're ready for, and that influences me to improve every day. I wouldn't like to be the factor holding someone back from massive success or to miss an opportunity for my team to teach me.

How has your business adapted to having a family?

My family is my world. I hope that one day when my children are old enough, they look at the life they possess and see a mother who worked hard, dreamt big, and taught them to chase their dreams. Of course, this is a concept I get from my parents' influence and their effort to give their children a great life. With everything I do in my business, my family is in my heart and mind. In hindsight, I know the gift of network marketing was given to me, so I could be home with my daughter, and future children, to experience all of their firsts.

I now run my business around my daughter. I'm present in her life every day and can complete activity when she is sleeping. She doesn't miss me for two hours in an evening, as she's in bed. I can have business meetings with her present if needed. I can coach and inspire from my lounge room with her playing with her toys. How many multimillion-dollar businesses can you run with your children in your arms? The flexibility of network marketing is key when building a business. I'm lucky I also have a supportive family that helps me when needed. Since becoming a mum, the best thing I've learnt is to focus on the things you can do, not what you can't, and make that work!

Your top five tips for an aspiring GEN Y to succeed in network marketing?

1. TREAT YOUR BUSINESS LIKE A BUSINESS.

   I know that sounds so simple, however, when I first came into the network marketing field, I said yes and hoped for the best. I listened to my sponsors, did what they asked me to do, and then thought I was lucky to have the success I was having.

I knew my work ethic was second to none, but I had no idea what I was doing, and I did try and get away with every shortcut possible. In my mind, I was classing it as an innovation. I was excited about the opportunity but shy about asking others to take a look. I loved the product but thought I would be annoying to share it with others. I got my sponsors to speak to people for me, as I had, and still do have, a fear of the phone. It turned out to be a huge weakness for me to move forward.

I wanted to be at the top of the company but didn't have the skills to get there, and then I wondered why it was taking me so long to become "successful." Yep I wanted to be a top leader in my company without speaking to anyone or improving my weaknesses. It sounds ridiculous, doesn't it?

I feel so fortunate to have found Eric Worre. I can't sing his praises enough. Whenever I have a new business partner, I always ask them to listen to his audio book and learn the skills it takes to become a network marketing professional. Mr Worre's live events are on my bucket list to attend. I can't wait to express my gratitude in person as he teaches that if you set your goals from the viewpoint of growth and contribution you can be at the top and help others to be there as well. I feel he has no agenda other than helping others to be successful in network marketing, and I aspire to be a selfless leader like he is.

2. DON'T COMPARE YOURSELF TO OTHERS.

This is hard to do when we're so great at recognition in network marketing. Take away the timeline. So many people get started, and they say they'll give it six months. Yes, it's important to have goals and aim high, but by removing the timeline it's going to free up your mind to have peace and contentment in the here and now. Rather than having an attitude that you must reach a certain title by a specific date, replace that with the message, "I will until." This will allow you to be present in your business, and it's more attractive to everyone you're sharing your business with.

3. HAVE DETERMINATION AND RESILIENCE.

Your determination has to be greater than the process. Distractions, frustrations, and setbacks are always going to be there. When you make your purpose greater, you can work through the hurdles. Think through what your greater purpose is as to why you started your network marketing business. The bigger vision for your life and not just your reasons for running your business day to day when it is convenient. Your business is going to be the vehicle to realise your purpose. What is that for you?

4. HAVE INTEGRITY.

In a small country town, if I, or one of my business partners, did something dishonest, everyone would find out instantly. If you always complete your business with integrity, positivity, and care, then nine times out of ten your team will, too. People always remember how you make them feel, not what you say. In my business I get paid by helping others look and feel fabulous, and to have an unwavering belief that everyone can live the life of their dreams, because they're worth it!

5. YOU ATTRACT INTO YOUR LIFE OF WHAT YOU THINK ABOUT MOST.

If you're happy, bubbly, caring, and wanting the best for your business partners and clients, you're going to get that back ten-fold. Be aware of your thoughts and place value on being positive and energising. When you walk into a room, light it up. Don't dim it with negativity. Don't worry. I'm not saying you have to be happy all of the time. There will be moments when life happens. Awareness of being solution focused and positive will help your journey. In the end, achieving your dreams without people who are caring, happy, and want the best for you, is empty. Achieve and live the life of your dreams, but do it through helping others.

Thank you for reading my journey, so far! I hope I get to meet you and inspire you to take a step towards your dream, because YOU ARE WORTH IT!

CHAPTER 5

Steph Bartram

"I AM. Two of the most powerful words. For what you put after them shapes your reality."

Unknown

CHAPTER FIVE

Steph Bartram

What is your background?

When asked to tell my story, I used to think it was kind of boring compared to many of the other amazing women I've met in the network marketing Industry. I come from a 'traditional' family and did the 'traditional' education thing and went to uni, really just for the fun of it, because I still had no idea what I wanted to *be* in life. Then I followed the 'traditional' process of getting a job, getting married, and having children. But when I reflect deeply on what my journey has been like, and I look around at what I've experienced and created, I realise I've actually spent my entire life challenging the 'traditional' path and searching and striving for the extraordinary. And the life I live now and the people in it are exactly that.

High school for me was very much about rebelling the 'traditional high-achieving schoolgirl' path my parents knew I could easily have followed. I was pretty smart but also loved to socialise. People and learning were my passions. I was constantly battling my love of social experiences with my talent for academic challenge. These loves clashed, because the people I was drawn to or connected with socially were not into learning or dreaming of big futures like I was. As a result, I often played down my intelligence in front of friends. I loved being in relationships with people who were probably labelled as 'strugglers.' These relationships taught me so much and challenged my ideas and perspectives. They made me feel strongly about equality and opportunity for all. I used to really challenge the teachers I thought were doing a mediocre job for my struggling friends who were being left behind.

I started to build this little part inside of me that really wanted to make a difference and help others. But it battled with the other part that had a powerful business mind and a strong drive to achieve something big. I then spent the next ten years figuring out how to channel those different energies and passions into something that could provide me personal fulfilment and wealth.

A defining event I will never forget was when I wanted to run for School Captain in Year 12. I always loved the concept of leadership, and I knew I could do a great job. But I didn't fit into the traditional box of school captains, I think mainly because I liked to challenge the status quo, push the boundaries, and break some rules. I was told by the school that I couldn't run, because I would be voted in based on popularity and not because of the job that I would do! This really cut me deep but sparked something in me to prove I could be smart and successful, whilst also maintaining relationships with whomever I chose. This is where my drive began. This was when I decided I would not allow anyone to limit what I could achieve, the positive impact I could leave on the world, and how many lives I could change.

I actually ended up doing quite well in Year 12. I think everyone was surprised but me. I remember I wanted to do a course in entrepreneurship, but I assumed I wasn't good enough or creative enough for that. No one pushed me to explore it further, as it was a bit outside of the box back then. So I ended up studying a Double Degree in Sports Science and Business at uni. I'm not sure why I chose human movement, because I'm fairly uncoordinated, but maybe it was because I enjoyed hanging out with sporty people. I think it's their energy and drive that I really connect with. And fancy that, I ended up marrying a PE teacher!

So off I went on the traditional path of getting a job. After a few different career changes I ended up becoming a teacher. I loved the relationships and mentoring side of teaching, but I really just wanted to teach students how to know themselves, reflect, develop their confidence and resilience, and help them dream big, so they could be valuable, contributing members of the community. But that subject has yet to make it into the curriculum.

I quickly realised what I was searching for didn't exist in the job world, and I would constantly ask myself what I could do to create a change and work for myself. It was when I was on maternity leave with my first child that the urgency of working for myself and having flexible hours became a high priority, and an opportunity fell right into my lap! When I realised there was a way to live without alarm clocks, limitations on income, limitations on dreams, and limitations on time, it was like I was awake in my life again.

When my best friend called me to tell me about this network marketing business opportunity, I could see it was a defining moment. It was the combination of my two passions coming together to provide me with a life of fulfilment, wealth, and freedom. I could see the big picture. I didn't even think about *how* I would make it work. I just saw the reasons *why* I had to make it work. My love for people and my love for learning were coming together in the form of a flexible, limitless entrepreneurial opportunity.

Growing up, I always dreamt big, worked hard, and knew I was meant for something great. But I never thought it would come packaged up as a network marketing business. Who even knows what network marketing is when you're at school making career decisions? But here we are, three years into my career in an industry I had no idea even existed, and I've never felt more like my authentic self or been more fulfilled and excited for the future.

Who inspires and influences you?

My Husband, Drew, is a massive influence in my life. The great Jim Rohn says, "You are a product of the five people you surround yourself with most." I'm happy to say Drew is my number one, and that has a positive impact on me both personally and professionally. Before we were married, when we were young, wild, and free, we developed a relationship motto that we lived by, which is, *You are your own person.*

This motto has served us well. It has allowed us both to grow and develop as supported individuals in our relationship and to create a life we love together. "You are your own person" prompts us to ask ourselves:

"Is this what I want?"

"Is this where I want to go?"

"Can I be responsible for that decision?"

And then we come together to plan, organise, compromise if required, and figure out how to make it happen in our family unit. Drew's a fun guy who lives in the moment and has an affectionate temperament that balances my more structured, driven, and factual personality. He's always challenging himself, and that inspires me to be my best as well. This year he ran the Auckland Marathon and raised money for our local hospital. I thought that was so freakin' amazing, and it made me so proud and grateful to have such an inspirational sidekick in life.

My mum is a teacher, and my dad's a farmer/accountant/business owner. My parents always told me I would be destined for something great and encouraged me to try new things. They instilled in me the belief that every new experience is an opportunity to grow and learn. When I pulled crazy stunts like changing my university plans to follow some boy I met at Schoolies, they allowed me to fall on my own feet and learn my own lessons along the way. When Drew and I packed all of our belongings in the car and headed west without much of a plan, Mum encouraged me to go and see what happens. "If you don't like it, the world won't end," she said. "You can always make a change." Wise lady.

I'm absolutely inspired every day by the people in my team, as well as others in the industry. When someone in my team challenges themselves to achieve something great in their business, I can hear a new strength in their tone of voice. They grow, their confidence soars, and they hold their head a little higher. I love being a part of that, and it inspires me to be better. The stories of the amazing women who've come before me in the industry, inspire me to keep jumping over the hurdles, to keep challenging the status quo, and to keep moving forward.

I'm always thinking about how my actions and words influence the way my children view the world and themselves. They inspire me to always do my best, stand up for what I believe in, and be a strong and proud woman. Just yesterday I was unloading the car and was taking one of the twins out first, when my eldest started whining to get out. I said in a huff, "I can't get everyone out at once. I'm not a superwoman!" to which she so innocently replied, "But yes you are, Mummy!" It stopped me in my tracks. It's not about being a *superwoman* as a label or being superior to others, but it's about knowing my daughter wholeheartedly and unwaveringly believes I can do some pretty amazing things. That's what's important to me.

Finally, I think you have to be inspired by yourself. I love this quote: "Be yourself. Unless you can be a unicorn, In that case, you should always be a unicorn." If you're striving to be someone else, it's like wishing you were a unicorn. It's impossible, and you'll always be disappointed with the result. So be true to your authentic self, inspire yourself, and *be* the change you want to see in your world.

What has been your biggest hurdle in the network marketing business?

An intelligent human once said, "The biggest hurdle in life is getting over yourself." High five to that! I don't know who said this, but it totally rings true for me. Never in a million years did I think I would end up selling skincare, nutrition, and makeup for a living, and in the beginning of my business journey the old *judgy-wudgy* Steph took a while to be proud of doing exactly that. My mind would say things like, *Oh, don't speak to Sally about this. She's an accountant. She won't be interested.* Or, *Steph, it's impossible to make as much money selling lipstick as you do being a teacher.* But I kicked the old Steph to the curb the only way I knew how. By empowering myself through learning. I learned how to apply makeup and take care of my skin. I learned how to confidently speak in front of a room of grown women. I learned that to be successful, I must feed my mind daily with positivity. I learned the stories of some of the most inspirational and successful women in the network marketing industry and built the belief that I could be one of them. I learned to share the gift I had in offering people my company's products and business opportunity. And in the wise words of Taylor Swift I learned to *shake it off* when things don't go to plan or life throws me a curveball.

The wonderful thing about hurdles is you can jump right over them and keep moving forward. Do you know what I think about when I'm having a moment where my ego is getting in the way of my business? I think about what would have happened if my best friend had never offered this business to me. What if she thought to herself, *I won't tell Steph about this, because she's not really into makeup, so I'm sure she wouldn't be interested.* I would be devastated if I found out she had an opportunity to impact my family's life, but she was too afraid to share it with me in case I said no.

I'm so unbelievably grateful to Jess for literally gifting me the opportunity to change my family's life. So when it feels like the haters are hating, and I'm slipping into that zone where I'm making it all about myself and not about the lives I can change, I get out of my own way and get offering.

What's it like to be a busy mum and run a network marketing business?

Having three children in under two years wasn't really in the original master plan, so boy was I grateful for this business when I was told we were having twins. More than ever, I needed flexibility, time leverage, and two income streams just to pay for all of those nappies. This is how we roll in our house to make it possible for me to be a Mumpreneur:

- Routine and Planning

  I live in a world of organised chaos. I do all of the organizing, and everyone else around me creates the chaos. It seems to work well. I created a diary/planner that works for me. I use my planner like my bible. If it's not written in my planner, it will never happen. I've always been into routine and daily habits, as I seem to be most productive, and least stressed, when there's a time and place for everything.

- Commitment and Consistency

  Even when I'm exhausted, because my kids are sick or I don't feel like I can get off the couch, because I've been running around like a headless chook all day, I do what I promised I was going to do. I don't cancel. I don't say, "I'll do it tomorrow." I just commit to doing what I need to do to grow my business and get it done. Having said that, I always prioritise my life and only commit to what aligns with my values and what I know I can achieve. Bite-sized chunks every day, consistently, is my strategy. Over-committing and then letting myself, or others, down is far worse than recognising I simply can't do everything and have to say no to what doesn't take me toward my goals.

- Vision and My *Why*

  When you have a clear picture in your head of what you want, and have an emotional connection to why you want it, the *how* will just happen. My vision and my *why* are strong enough to get me over the hurdles and to keep me moving forward when life isn't flowing as easily as I'd like it to. And when my *why* is staring up at me in the form of three little people every morning, I'm reminded to be a strong, independent, and proud role model.

- Support at Home

  My husband is a pretty top bloke, and we've always been a partnership in life. We run with the motto, *You are your own person* and support each other in achieving our goals by splitting chores and responsibilities evenly between us. We both have careers, and we both had a hand in creating our children, therefore we're equally responsible for how they're raised and what's for dinner tonight. We have honest conversations about where we're at and how we can best support one another when life gets a bit hectic. It's not always rainbows and butterflies, but we're a team, and we both foster and support each other's passions and dreams.

- Imperfection

  I'm fine with being imperfect. I prioritise and then let some things go for the day. Mostly domestic duties, which aren't really my forte. I focus on progress rather than perfection. Get out of your head and get it done, and then move on.

What rewards and recognitions have you received?

To be really honest, I've never been one to be driven by public reward or recognition. My husband will tell you I'll run a mile from anything that resembles a competition. Dangle a carrot in front of me, and my body will shut down. I like to quietly compete with myself to be the best I can be, but that's about as far as it goes. Even writing this section of my chapter I can feel myself getting uncomfortable reeling off the rewards I've earned in network marketing.

I've learnt one important thing about myself in this business. I absolutely thrive on being personally recognised in private for a job well done by people I respect. A note from a team member to say thanks for supporting them, a conversation with my husband where he tells me how proud he is of me, and having a wine with my best girlfriends where they tell me I'm a positive role model for my daughters. That's what drives me.

Having said that, I have to admit it's kind of funny, because despite feeling awkward about it, I have earned quite a few rewards in this business. In my first few months I earned free flights to the annual conference. Then I earned a spa incentive to spend the day with my upline, the top earner in my company in Australia. I've earned annual family holidays paid for by the company to Fiji and the Gold Coast, a Mercedes Benz, a watch, and Tiffany & Co jewellery. All of which I've thoroughly enjoyed and am extremely grateful for.

I do love the company I'm with because of how thoughtful they are. They send me flowers for my birthday, which keeps my husband on his toes, flowers for Australia Day, Tiffany's for Christmas, and a thoughtful gift for Valentine's Day. It's always nice to feel special.

What's the biggest difference between teaching and the network marketing business?

I can honestly say that I loved being in the classroom with the teenagers of the world. They challenged me, my perspective, and my values, and kept me on my toes. If teaching was just about going to school and working with teenagers to help them become the best versions of themselves, that would be a gig I could have stuck with.

But the teaching profession/education system just wasn't creative or flexible enough for me to feel fulfilled. I've always thought that if only there was a subject called *Being Awesome at Life* I would love to teach it. That's where I see my value in contributing to the community, and that's what I've been able to now create outside of the school environment, with the network marketing opportunity.

I found that network marketing filled in those gaps where teaching left me feeling deflated. It combined the aspects I loved about teaching with the challenges and environment I needed to thrive. What I loved about teaching was the relationships, mentoring, role modelling, increasing the confidence of others to strive and dream outside the box, time management, responsibility, self-reflection, and my own learning and growing. I've been able to transfer these straight across to my network marketing business. What deflated me were all of the meetings, hours and hours of after-school and weekend work without any compensation, and the red tape and limitations as to what we were able to do. The limited resources made it difficult to impact lives like I wanted to.

With network marketing. I was able to run my business with my authentic personality and values at the forefront. The more effort I put in, the more I was compensated. I could be creative in my approach and work my business flexibly to suit my lifestyle. I could schedule meetings when it suited me, and I could manage the tone of my business. I loved that everyone I worked with was there because they wanted to be, and with the intention of helping others and being the best version of themselves. The culture I've created as a result is one that promotes success. So I suppose the major difference is the freedom to be / have / do things the way I want to and when I want to.

What are the daily tasks essential to your network marketing business?

Because I run my business from home with my kids around all of the time, I really have to plan and prioritise how I work my time. I block out thirty minutes non-negotiable each day when the kids are asleep to do personal tasks like business conversations, filling my calendar, and following up. The rest is all completed in the spare moments here and there or in the evenings when my kids are asleep. That's when I work with my team via virtual software, so they can be anywhere in the world, and we're still connected.

I honestly just do what I can with the time that I have on the given day. I'm all about consistency. If you're doing something every day that's building your business, you will move forward. That's the key.

I do personal development every day, because I'm a bit of a self development junkie. Reading books, listening to audios, watching clips, and attending conferences or women's leadership events. Whatever I can do to up my skills and grow myself, to add more value to others is super important to me. Keeping your mind filled with positive thoughts is vital to growing a business from home. I see it all of the time in myself and in my team. If someone isn't doing their personal development, it shows in the results.

You have to smile and laugh every day. Even when you feel like nothing is worth smiling about. Find a way. Watch a YouTube clip or look at photos of yourself from when you were sixteen, although that might result in more cringing than laughing. Roll around on the floor with your kids, or do something really nice for a random stranger. That's the stuff that gets the good energy beaming out of you, and this is when people are attracted to you and want to be around you. Smiling and laughing are absolutely essential to daily business.

What does your future look like?

Today we have three children under three. We live in our brand-new home in a small country town, and I choose how I spend my time. I don't miss out on precious moments with my children, I don't sacrifice my drive and professional passions, I don't spend time worrying about how I'm going to pay my bills, and I don't wonder if I'll ever get to do what I want. Because with this business, I have that all covered.

Now I spend my time creating, supporting others, building, growing, learning, role modelling, enjoying the right now, and planning my family's future with intent and excitement. When I think about what I wanted my life to look like when I started this business three years ago, this is certainly on the right track. I'm so grateful I was offered this business and had the openness and confidence to accept it and commit to its journey.

Providing my children with experiences that will open their minds, feed their souls, and touch the lives of others, has always been important to me, so we look forward to a lot of travel and experiences as a family in the future.

My husband and I spent a couple of years in the Kimberley and have a real passion for Aboriginal culture and education, so we'd love to get back up there again at some stage.

We've just built our first family home, so lots of special memories are going to be created there.

I continue to grow and nurture my network marketing business and support as many other people as I possibly can to be successful in creating the life they truly desire through this super-smart business model.

What's your advice for people who say they have no time?

I seriously get a heavy heart when people open up and share with me how unhappy they are in their current financial situation, but feel they don't have enough time to do anything to change it. I often hear, "I wish I could, but..." It upsets me that people give up so easily on something they truly want. It's sad, because for whatever reason, people feel the need to make time their excuse for not pursuing their dream, when deep down they know it's not true. They don't believe in themselves enough to receive an opportunity for change. The fear of failure, or even fear of success, is paralysing them, and they don't have the confidence to say yes to something they know truly has the power to change their life. And honestly, that sucks!

Here's an interesting fact: Beyoncé has the same twenty-four hours in her day as the rest of us, and how freaking amazing is she? You can be amazing as well. Seriously. Whatever amazing looks like for you, it's possible. You can have that. What can you create if you just start to prioritise your time, get yourself sorted, and with some focus and strategy, commit to consistency and personal growth, and then just get to work on making it happen?

This is a little bit *woo-woo*, but I love using afformations, which are not to be confused with affirmations, to help move past mental blocks about time. Afformations are empowering questions that change your subconscious thought patterns. You can ask yourself this question whenever you feel overwhelmed by time: *Why do I have so much time to do all of the things I want to do?* This will prompt the brain to go searching for all of the ways you have to create time for what you want. It might sound crazy, but hey, it works.

I love that the network marketing industry allows you to *earn* while you *learn*. Nobody knows what they're doing when they first enter this business, but you can start earning right from the outset. Then as you grow and learn, your earnings will follow. It's flexible in terms of when you choose to work your business around your other commitments. Making a few 'sacrifices' like not watching TV in the evenings, and to instead commit your time to building your business in the short term, will long be forgotten when you've created long-term financial and time freedom for yourself and your family.

So, if you have *no time* to build something that's going to provide you with all of the time in the world in the future, to me just doesn't make any sense. If you think time is your issue, I encourage you to delve deeper into yourself and figure out what's really stopping you from creating change. Once you address it, you can start moving forward towards creating the life you choose.

What are your five tips for people looking to get into the network marketing business?

1. IF YOU FOLLOW THE SYSTEM AND GROW YOURSELF, YOU WILL BE SUCCESSFUL.

   This business is simple but not easy. It's about consistently doing what you need to do when no one is watching over your shoulder or making you do it. That's the hard part. Being accountable to yourself. It's about the one-percenters. It's about committing to however long it takes. If you want something that's going to make you wealthy overnight, or you think you might go and sit on a boat and drink champagne after month two in your business, this industry is probably not for you.

2. ASK QUESTIONS, AND RESEARCH THE COMPANY'S OFFICIAL DOCUMENTATION.

   And I don't mean 'Google it.' Some of the rubbish I read on Google about my company is beyond ridiculous. Everyone thinks their company is the best, and it probably is for them. Find a company with some products you like, a sponsor who has similar values to yours, and you have yourself a winning recipe right there. If you're selling something you enjoy using, you're a product of your product, and you're working with people you enjoy being around, then you're on the right track for sure.

3. JUST DO IT.

    Once you let the doubt and negativity creep in, which can happen at lightning speed, your dreams are on the backburner. Don't think about the *how*, just do it. Nike didn't become one of the most recognised brands in the world by sitting around thinking their 'tick' might not be what some people want or their shoes might not be useful to everyone. Back yourself and take some action. Just start somewhere and figure out the rest as you go. Every day counts, and if you're waiting for some magical moment for everything to be just right, you're wasting your days.

4. BE STRONG ENOUGH TO MAKE THE DECISION FOR YOURSELF, KNOWING IT'S WHAT'S BEST FOR YOU AND YOUR FAMILY.

    There will be people who will try to hold you back, put you down, or deter you, but they aren't the ones paying your bills, planning the futures of your children, or living life through your soul, so make sure, you do what's right for you, knowing you will find a new tribe of people who are likeminded, supportive, and cheering you on toward your goals and dreams. Haters gonna hate, but they ain't gonna pay your bills or live in your shoes!

5. DON'T BE GUIDED BY FEAR.

    Let yourself dream again. It's not about pretending you don't have fears. Fear of failure, fear of success, fear of what others will say, fear of being pushy or salesy, or fear of losing money. We all have fears, but it's about overcoming them by making your dreams even bigger than the fears. Ask yourself what your life will look like in five years from now if you don't make a change.

"You are good enough, smart enough, beautiful enough, strong enough. Believe it, and never let insecurity run your life."

Thema Davis

CHAPTER 6

Chelsea Dolby

CHAPTER SIX

Chelsea Dolby

What is your background? When did you realize what you wanted to do with your life?

I was lucky I always knew I wanted to work in the beauty industry when I was at school. A lot of my friends didn't have a clue what career they wanted to pursue, even when they were at university. I knew I never wanted to go to university, and so when I was in Year 12 I started working at a local beauty salon after school and loved it.

I was also lucky enough to start fulltime after I finished high school and learn the trade from my boss instead of going off to a private beauty college. Over the years I developed my skills, completed different courses, became experienced in the field, and eventually went to college to complete my Diploma in Beauty Therapy.

I left Horsham and moved to Torquay in my early twenties, where I worked in a couple of salons before I branched into the medical cosmetic industry working for a couple of plastic surgeons. Over the years I endorsed many different products and services whilst continuing to love the industry.

What I didn't love was being told what I was worth per hour and that I wasn't getting paid enough for my worth. I was brought up as a hard worker. My first job was at a catering business at the age of thirteen. I've always had pride and a great work ethic and gone above and beyond what was required of me.

I would go to work at the salons and clinics early and leave late after cleaning up, but I never got extra income for it. I worked especially hard over Christmas and summer holiday periods and was lucky to even get a Christmas card, let alone a big, fat bonus at the end of the year to say thanks for all you do.

What I also didn't like that I was told when I could have holidays. I love the warm weather and especially living on the coast over summer. I hardly ever got to experience it, as we were never allowed to have holidays during that time of year. I felt restricted and not in control of my life. I loved what I did, but I didn't love working for someone else.

I always knew I was destined for something more than to be an employee for the rest of my life. I was sick of working hard to make someone else rich. I began to wonder what would happen if I could put in that much effort to make myself rich. My entrepreneurial spirit and desire to create more in my life was always there, and I knew I would have my own business someday.

What did you do to make your dream a reality?

After having my first child, Jett, and being home fulltime with him, I look back and realize I had signs of postnatal depression. I felt I had nothing of value or interest to contribute to anyone. I was just a stay-at-home Mum. Who would want to talk to me??

I also wasn't financially contributing to the household, which I struggled with, as I had always done what I wanted with the money I earned. To ask for money off my partner and justify what I was spending it on, was tough.

I felt unfulfilled, as I had lost my identity and independence. However, I also felt guilty that I was having these feelings, because I loved being a mum to Jett and spending time with him.

This was when I had a fabulous idea to follow my dream and start my own beauty salon. I had identified a gap in the market for a salon at a small coastal town nearby and discovered a development of retail shops in the perfect location. I spoke with the developer and started planning my new venture. I didn't know how I was going to finance this business, but I had suddenly found a way for my dreams to become a reality, and I vowed I would find a way.

I had everything mapped out, from the name to the layout. I'd done all of the research. Then right up to just about the point of completion, the developer decided to lease the shop to another interested person instead, as she was financially more stable than I was.

How did you get into network marketing?

I was absolutely shattered at the time. I felt my dream bubble had burst, and all of the time and effort I'd put into creating my own business was for nothing.

This project had sparked something in me and pulled me out of the funk I had gotten into. I was going to become that independent, successful business person I knew I was destined to be.

Looking back, I now understand I couldn't see what was about to unfold for me. Some call it coincidence, while others call it fate. I'm a strong believer in the universe and that everything happens for a reason, because it was not long after this devastating time I was introduced to a network marketing business that was brand new to Australia.

I'd never heard of network marketing before and must admit that when I was sitting in the kitchen with my gorgeous friend, Ali, and she was telling me about her friend, Vanessa, who'd just started a Swiss skincare and cosmetics business, I immediately thought of party plan companies. My mum had been involved in one before, so I had the preconceived ideas about what this was about. A room full of women sitting around a kitchen table or lounge room, playing games and trying products on the back of their hands.

My ego was telling me there was no way I would lower myself to do something like this. I had worked in professional salons and medical clinics, I wasn't going to knock on doors and drop off catalogues!

It wasn't until Ali mentioned you could earn a brand-new white Mercedes and five-star holidays for you and your family that my ears pricked up. I decided to meet up with Vanessa, who proceeded to tell me more about the company and products, and I'm so pleased I let go of all of the preconceived ideas and fears I had and was open minded enough to listen to what she had to say.

Being a beauty therapist, I was eager to experience and research the products to discover how good they actually were, as I wouldn't be able to promote something I wasn't passionate about. As it turned out, these products, in my opinion, are the best I've ever worked with, and I've worked with quite a few over the years.

I also gained more knowledge about the business model and soon discovered it ticked all of the boxes I was looking for in a business and much more. At this time in my life I was pregnant with my second child, so starting a business from home, with such low start-up costs, while having the flexibility to be present with my two year old, sounded like a perfect combination.

Right away, I invested in some business tools I didn't have to get a bank loan to purchase and started talking to my network of family and friends. Even though I had very little knowledge of the products and company, the majority could hear the excitement in my voice and see the spark reignite within me, so they were quite supportive.

Some weren't so encouraging, which was disappointing, but I soon realized it was a part of the process. Not everyone is going to be open to a different business model. I believe it isn't for everybody, and people can choose to have a negative opinion, even when they don't have all of the facts.

My business soon started to build, and when I gave birth to my daughter, Lotti, I was receiving a regular income every month. My team had started growing, and although I had a newborn and a three year old, I was still able to run my business, coach my team, and develop my skills from the comfort of my home, all thanks to the internet.

As time went on, my sponsor decided to step back from the business due to personal reasons. I continued to grow my business but eventually started feeling a bit lost and looking for direction, when I decided to take it to the next level.

This is when I was so grateful for the beautiful leader in our organization, Debbie Loughnane, who reached down and took me under her wing. I had been attending every training and event she'd organized and was constantly active in my business, so she could see the potential in me. I started working closely with Debbie as she regularly mentored and coached me. I was also introduced to personal development for the first time, which I embraced, and it immediately started to change my world.

I had never done any personal development before, and soon my confidence and leadership skills grew, which increased my business. This also gave me an insight into the confidence, self-esteem, and self-worth I had lost at home with an unsupportive partner.

I was in a relationship where I felt I couldn't be myself, because I was constantly being made into something else. Something that wasn't me.

So I'm thankful for investing in personal development, because it empowered me to go on a journey of self-discovery to realise how much I let myself be controlled into feeling I was small and worthless.

From when I first decided to start my own network marketing business, I was told I was spending too much money on it, I was never at home, and I always put my business before my family. Ironically, the reason I was building this business was to provide for my family and have the flexibility to be there for them. I was earning a corporate income without spending the corporate hours away from home and having someone else raising my children.

I would leave our company events feeling on top of the world, my confidence, self-esteem, and energy soaring after people came up to me to let me know how inspiring and amazing I was, only to have my energy come crashing down when I got home, due to the negative comments and put downs.

With the business giving you confidence, but your home life doing just the opposite, something had to change, right?

A pivotal point occurred two and a half years into my business when the consistent activity and helping others to achieve their goals allowed me to promote to the third management level within the company and earned me my very own white Mercedes. I was the fourth one in our organization to attain this achievement, and the first of a long list of successful people to start promoting out. I was proud I could show others it was possible and inspire them to also achieve it.

This was such a critical goal I had created for myself and felt a deep sense of accomplishment. I wasn't going to allow anyone to be a dream stealer. I had grown and developed so much, nothing was going to stop me. I was the confident, strong, laser-focused woman I desired to be with a *no-matter-what* attitude!

I soon realised my home situation was toxic to me and my children, so I was able to empower myself. I also developed the confidence to empower others and to build a business that gave me the financial independence to eventually leave that situation. I knew I could support myself and my children and have the freedom to become the best version of myself while creating a new, positive, and happy environment for us all.

I see women who choose to stay in an unhappy, toxic relationship, because they're financially dependent on their partner, and it saddens me. I had the courage to choose something different, which ended up giving me my life back, thanks to the choice I made to start my own network marketing business. It's my objective to inspire and share my story with anyone who's also looking to make a change.

How were you able to build your business while being a single mum?

Being a single mum of two kids, I was able to continue building my business by working when the kids spent time with their dad. This was every second weekend and a couple of nights during the week. Having a network marketing business permitted me to be flexible.

It also then allowed me to be a hundred percent present with my kids when they were with me, which was critical to me during this major transition in their lives. I was so grateful I had the flexibility to pick and choose when I worked and when I didn't.

Another amazing incentive I could earn by building my business is incredible five-star holidays every year for you and your family. I was lucky enough to have earned these holidays every year since I started my business but hadn't taken advantage of the opportunity for different reasons, until I became a single mother.

I was determined to earn a family holiday to Port Douglas for myself and the kids, because I wanted them to share in the rewards my hard work and commitment could offer them. They were so excited to fly on a plane up to

Port Douglas. When we pulled into the Sea Temple Resort, their eyes lit up with amazement. The one memory that will always be etched in my mind is the look on their faces as we opened the door to our two-bedroom apartment we'd be staying in for the week.

We had our own pool, and the apartment was bigger and way more luxurious than the house we were living in at the time. This was why I was building my business. So my kids could have a life full of choices, fun, and incredible experiences. That holiday was exactly what we needed, and I would have never been able to afford it if it wasn't for my network marketing business.

The kids have since been fortunate enough to go to Fiji on another luxurious resort holiday. They've developed fantastic relationships with other kids in our organization and have so many memories and amazing experiences, thanks to my business.

After being a single mum for just over a year, I was so happy when the universe once again weaved its magic, and I reconnected with the love of my life one day over coffee.

Matt and I grew up in Horsham and first became romantically involved when we were eighteen. Over the years, we were in and out of each other's lives. I always made sure I found out what he was up to, as he was always in my heart. I knew he'd brought a business in Geelong seven years previous but hadn't caught up in that time. So one night on Facebook I contacted him and organized to meet for coffee the following day.

From the moment I saw him walk into the café, I got butterflies in my stomach and knew this was going to be different from all of the previous catch-ups we'd have had. And I was right. This soon developed into an incredible relationship, and for the first time I felt I could be me, wholeheartedly, and not be criticized for it.

He's so supportive of whatever I do, loves me for me, and empowers me to be the best version of myself. He raises me up, validates and admires my strengths and skills, challenges me, and brings valuable suggestions to the table. He's so positive and funny and brings out the best in me. When I realized I found my true love, it allowed me to really understand myself.

He's incredible with the kids. His love and loyalty to them is unquestionable, and he treats them as if they were his own. It's beautiful to see the love and respect the kids have for him in return. This was an important aspect for me when it came to introducing another male father figure, as I wanted my kids to grow up in a loving, secure, happy household.

What is your life like now?

I finally feel like I have my life together, and I'm a hundred percent satisfied and happy. After an amazing holiday in New York and Las Vegas in April of 2015, another dream came true, and Matt asked me to marry him in front of some of my closest friends at the Bellagio Fountains in Vegas. We were married on December 13, 2015 on a beach at Point Roadknight and partied all night close by. The day I married my soul mate was perfect and incredible.

Who has inspired and influenced you in your life and business, and why?

The first person I want to mention is my amazing mentor, friend, and business partner, Debbie Loughnane. As I mentioned earlier, she was the one who saw the potential in me way before I saw it for myself. She poured so much belief into me when I didn't believe in myself and lifted me up. She was my support, especially in the dark times. Her phenomenal business and achievements has led the way and shown us all what's possible. I will be forever grateful for her generosity, kindness, and knowledge, and I love her unconditionally.

My mum, Noela Hair, has been a major influence and inspiration to me. She has always put my brother and me before herself. In fact, she puts almost everyone before herself. She's the most selfless person I know. Her dedication to her children and grandchildren is incredible.

She has instilled her hard work ethic into me. I remember her working three jobs, just so we wouldn't miss out on any opportunities growing up. I admire her strength I witnessed throughout the challenging time when she and my dad separated. She gave me the strength to step outside of my comfort zone and continue when I didn't think I had it in me.

She's always believed in me and been proud of everything I've done. She's stood by me even if she thinks I'm not making the right choice. I love her so much and will be happy if I'm half the mother to my children she is to me.

What are your three favourite things about network marketing?

The first is being in control of my life. I don't have a boss telling me how much I'm worth or when I have to work and when I can take holidays. If one of my kids is sick or has an excursion they require me to go to, I don't have to ring someone to ask if I can take a day off.

The flexibility and freedom has been a vital factor that has allowed me to build a business and create a corporate income, whilst dealing with life's curveballs.

The opportunity to travel and holiday at least twice a year is definitely a highlight for me and my family. I was reflecting recently about how many five-star holidays we can earn just by building our businesses. I'm so grateful I have the opportunity to travel to the USA, plus holiday at incredible resorts throughout Australia and overseas every year. A majority of people are lucky to have a holiday every four or five years.

The last, and probably the most impactful part about network marketing I love, is being able to help change other people's lives. It's one thing to make a difference to your and your family's lives, but to be able to offer this amazing opportunity to someone else and see how it changes their life is something words can't describe. I've changed the lives of so many people in my organization, because they had the courage to say yes to this opportunity to build their businesses and create their own life. It could be something as small as an extra $200 for a pair of shoes to a life-changing string of events for a family. I love that I can make a positive difference by inspiring and empowering others.

Do you have any suggestions for someone starting a network marketing business?

NEVER GIVE UP.

The only way to fail in this business is to give up.

There will be times when your will get knockbacks, people will be negative, and business partners will leave you, but the key is to not let it defeat you and to keep going. Everyone experiences these times in their businesses, including myself several times.

The best reward in a struggle is what you achieve at the other end, and I promise that if you never give up, you will be successful at your network marketing business. I've listened to many people who are top income earners and their stories of how they lost everything but had the strength and determination to rebuild their businesses, often on more than one occasion, to get to the level they're at today.

That's how leaders develop and grow. By learning from their mistakes and sharing what they've learnt to their team.

PLUG INTO EVERYTHING.

Make it your priority to attend every event, training, webinar and conference your company organises. The only way to go up is to show up. This is how I grew as a leader and developed the confidence to build my business and coach others to build theirs. You can't expect to grow your skills and knowledge by not learning from others in the industry. No matter how many times I go to a business presentation, I come away with something.

The fantastic aspect about network marketing is that you don't need to know anything to start your business. You get started, and then learn as you go. Be a sponge and give yourself the best possible advantage to start earning a measurable income by plugging into everything offered to you. You'll thank me later.

LEAVE YOUR EGO AT THE DOOR.

As I previously mentioned, I had an ego when I was first introduced to network marketing. I thought I was too good to be doing 'parties' and selling products to ladies. I soon realized my ego could have prevented me from creating the life I've always wished for.

Anyone, from any background, age, or experience can be successful at network marketing. To be humble and have integrity in everything you do is so important to create a successful business. It wouldn't matter if I was earning twenty dollars or $200,000 a month, I wouldn't treat anyone differently.

Everyone is watching you, so by being true to yourself and your organization, you will create a loyal and lasting culture. We're all the same and have the same opportunities to become successful. It's what you do with those opportunities that determines how much you'll achieve.

What does the future look like?

Over my journey I've learnt strength and resilience, which has allowed me to be confident and believe I deserved more, and so did my kids. They deserved the best mother they could have, and now they have her, along a loving, secure, and happy life.

Let me just end my story by revealing to you that I'm not a writer. Nor did I ever think in a million years I would be in a book. This is another incredible opportunity that has been presented to me because of network marketing. Nothing is impossible. If you can dream it, you can achieve it.

I've really struggled with writing this chapter and wanted to let you know that it has brought up a lot of raw emotions I'd put behind me and thought I'd dealt with. I didn't know how to turn what I had in my head into words on a page. Lots of moments I wanted to give up and not go ahead with it, especially after losing a day's work when my computer froze.

It would have been easy for me to just give up and quit, because I thought it was hard and way out of my comfort zone, but with the support and encouragement of my dear friend, Beck McIntyre, and my amazing new husband, I put on my big-girl panties and continued on. I realised I was no quitter! If I had given up when it all got too hard in by business and personal life, I wouldn't be where I am today, living the happy life I created.

I had the courage to step outside of my comfort zone and start my own network marketing business. To leave a toxic environment and create a better world for my kids and me, and to reunite with my soul mate who completes the person I am today.

I'll tell you what. If I can do it, anyone can. You can be and do whatever it is you want to, and don't let anyone tell you different. Believe in yourself, back yourself, and you can create anything!

Thank you.

"I am not afraid...I was born to do this."

Joan of Arc

Emily Loughnane

CHAPTER SEVEN

Emily Loughnane

What is your background, and how did you got into network marketing.

I was fourteen when network marketing began to change my life. A complete stranger from the other side of the world introduced my mum, ENVP Debbie Loughnane, to the industry. At this point in our lives, we were living week by week, just getting by and never getting to experience and live the life of total freedom and abundance we only dreamt of.

I grew up in a family that instilled a strong work ethic and belief in me, so I naturally developed an entrepreneurial spirit. Growing up around fashion, I'd only dreamt of becoming a designer. Throughout high school I worked hard to get the best possible score for my portfolios. I was exhausted and looking down the road to university. This is where I hoped I could tick the boxes of freedom, spontaneous living, and being a Gen Y boss. I had a big vision to break free from the traditional nine-to-five grind and be a part of a movement for the next generation of everyday people living out extraordinary lives. I knew my original Plan A was just not going to create that for me, and there was so much evidence around me that network marketing did work.

Being Australia's youngest Executive Regional Vice President, I feel so blessed to experience this early in my life. It means that at twenty one, I have the ability to cruise around in a white Mercedes with my green p plates and create a six-figure income with passion, profit, and purpose.

I consider myself the luckiest girl for being able to work alongside my mum, who has inspired me to be brave and breathe life into people like she has to me. We're closer now than ever. My little sister, Tayla Loughnane, joined our business when she turned eighteen, and I now get to pay this forward. The three of us build a business together as a family, and it has made my *why* even bigger, because it now includes inspiring her to succeed.

As a Gen Y's or twenty-somethings, we shouldn't be conditioned to being tired, exhausted, broke, overweight, and stressed. We shouldn't have to spend five days of a week working at a job that's not fulfilling and only enjoy two. I'm super-blessed to have built a business that allows other gen Y's to wake up every day without an alarm clock and be a lover of life. They get to predict what that day holds for them and truly design their own future. I so believe I'm at my happiest, because I get to sprinkle joy and kindness into people's lives just by choosing something different. Our life and our greatness should be celebrated daily.

There were times I didn't believe in myself, and I had to have a tough-love conversation with myself and ask if my target and dream were bigger than the lie of fear I kept telling myself. This is the part of the journey when I jumped in with both feet and took full responsibility for my business. I stepped into the space of becoming a driven leader and took ownership of what I was doing.

I remember when I was a little girl, Mum once said to me, "When you change, your whole world will change with you." That has stuck with me my whole life. I decided to invest in me and made a promise to grow and become the best version of myself. I decided to take this business seriously and be surrounded with likeminded and supportive people. Our thought patterns and mindset shape our reality every day.

I wake up every morning and ask myself, *So, what does my perfect day look like? What if I could do that every single day?* We Gen Y's have the mindset of wondering why we should work for another fifty-sixty years at a job we hate and then retire and start having fun at seventy. Why can't we start having fun right now?

The world is so conscious of what's happening around us. Whatever the normal was twenty or thirty years ago is now aging, and people are starting to wake up to knowing there has to be more. I know I felt that way. We all know someone who wants to create spontaneous living where you get on a plane that day just because you can or to create more choices. Who wouldn't love to create an additional income stream or live a happier, healthier, more abundant life? This business has been a vehicle for so many in my life, as well as my team, to create it. It's exciting times for the twenty-first century entrepreneur to be able to create a massive global business from anywhere in the world.

Who has inspired and influenced you, and why?

At the age of twenty two, I wake up every day and count my blessings by the people I've surrounded myself with and the mentors who bring out the best in me. I've always had a massive vision and a roaring, burning message inside of me that makes some people think I'm absolutely crazy. But I knew I had to grow myself and to have that vision I needed to be it and live it. To become that living example of everything I believed in and inspired me. The opportunity to grow as a twenty year old is the most amazing privilege in the world. In my three years as a young entrepreneur and professional network marketer, I've had a thirst for knowledge and am hungry to learn from the very best who've paved the way for me

Someone I've followed from the beginning of my journey is Gen Y Guru Michael McQueen. I was nineteen when I went to my first conference that inspired me to really see that Generation Y is the future of network marketing and to create sustainable success for the next fifty or sixty years, as they're always on the edge of technology and such forward thinkers. I could really see the importance of building networks with other likeminded Gen Y go-getters. Michael McQueen was someone who just spoke my language.

But I didn't get all of my lessons from one person. In network marketing, you grow from strength to strength with different experiences that require different lessons to be learnt. For example, when I needed to start growing my team I would listen to John Maxwell regarding leadership. Any time I needed to hear something about networking with my cold market I would listen to Eric Worre, or when I needed to be inspired I read someone like Oprah or Miranda Kerr.

My family has inspired me and moulded every inch of my being to play big in this world. I will forever be grateful to my beautiful dad, Tim Loughnane, for instilling a work ethic in me from the moment I turned thirteen. He came to my business presentations at the start of my business and sat in the car until I was done reading the trading post, because I was scared to drive on my own!

I will be forever be thankful for my little sister, Tayla Loughnane. who is one of the most authentic go-getters I've ever met, and she will never understand what her friendship and being my sidekick really means.

My stunning fiancé, Kane Allen, has grown with me from day one in this journey. He watched us go from living week by week eating frozen lasagne every night to now having the ability to building a life together. He is my number one fan. In a lot of relationships you either grow with each other or apart from one another, and he definitely has inspired me to choose an incredible life together.

My vibe that has attracted my tribe over the last three years with my success line made up of so many generations. Baby boomers, Gen X's and Gen Y bosses who've allowed me step into leadership that just gives me butterflies in my tummy, because they're changing their lives daily by teaching others how to do the same.

A big beautiful thank you to my leaders, ERVP Rachel Mau, RVP Amanda Holland, EAM Tarnee Rowan, AM Sammy Dobbin, AM Renae Boucher, AM Jamie-lee Clohsey, Tayla Loughnane, Jacquii Jackson, Chantelle Maher, Samantha Maloney, and Ruby Seiler.

Last, but not least, I absolutely believe to be a success in your network marketing business, you need to connect with amazing mentors who've paved the way, raised the bar, and really bring out your greatness. My mum, Debbie Loughnane, was that person for me. It had always been tough love in our house and everything we've worked towards. In most mother-daughter relationships, it's usually competition, but my mentor and mum chose empowerment.

What are your three favourite things about network marketing?

Wow, this is such a tough question, as it's so hard to pinpoint only three things I love about this industry, but I'll try to narrow it down. Here are my top three favourite things about network marketing, especially for someone who is a Generation Y, as it gives us the ability for it to be our vehicle to make a difference in the world. It allows us to earn more, so we can give more and set up the next generations coming through to choose something different from what we've always been conditioned to be.

1. Contributing to the world in bigger ways, which allows you to earn more and give more

2. Breaking free of the traditional nine to five, which allows all generations to rewrite their story

3. Paying it forward

What was your biggest hurdle in your network marketing business, and how did you overcome it?

I believe in business, and in life, everyone will go through their own lessons and allow themselves opportunities to grow. It will mostly happen when you're in the flow and are in momentum, and then you'll have that thing that will basically feel like it trips you up. For me, I'm sure you can already guess what that is. It was me. I was my very own obstacle, and it took me a little while to actually become aware of this.

Becoming a professional network marketer and entrepreneur when I was nineteen, I had this big sign across my forehead that read *I don't take myself seriously.* When I would meet people, that was the very first thing that they saw. So not only did I acknowledge what was going on, I had to have a tough-love conversation with myself to get it together. I told myself, *You know what you're capable of. You have a burning message inside of you that you need to share with the world.*

It was from that very moment I knew I was being the selfish one by holding myself back from becoming the invitation for other Gen Y's to explore what was possible. I became hungry for it and became a sponge for knowledge and for creating a business from entrepreneurs who'd paved the way for me. I loved listening to audios, reading books, and mirroring the people I would have loved to trade places with. According to millennials and a Future of Work survey, today, ninety percent of people believe that entrepreneurship is a mindset and fifty-eight percent of those are Generation Y.

I remember one specific day at the start of my journey when I was telling someone I didn't know very well, who was older than I was, about how much I loved personal development and leadership books. They just laughed directly in my face and said she couldn't believe I was nineteen and reading personal development books. For a long time I was always ashamed of having a thirst for knowledge and learning from the best, but I remember stopping myself and becoming aware of the two choices I had that day. One was to buy into her limited reality and cap myself from playing big or to become unapologetically me and step into the space of, *Get on my boat or get off my boat, but you're not stopping my boat.*

Three years later, I giggle at myself because of how easily I used to allow people to dictate what I was passionate about. We don't laugh at people when they want to get healthy and fit. We don't laugh when people take care of themselves when they're unwell. How is this any different? The days are gone when we stepped on each other to make ourselves feel better. Celebrate the people who surround you for their success and their happiness.

If you have a desire to better yourself and create more in your life, start with you. Read. Listen. Acknowledge. Believe and create. Because your mind will take you places where your butt could never dream of. Wouldn't it be amazing if girls could get more followers, because they were smart, funny, kind, inspiring, and brilliant versus just because of how perky their butt looked this week?

What does a day in the life of a Gen Y look like while running a network marketing business?

Not one day in the life of a Gen Y boss looks exactly the same, and I absolutely love that, as I'm so the opposite of routine. I love spontaneous living and going with the flow of what excites me for that day.

Okay, I want you to picture me with blonde hair that's slightly crazy, the biggest belly laugh, and very clumsy. I will explain my day for you.

As I'm fast asleep, tucked away in my bed at seven a.m., which is the middle of the night for me, my beautiful fiancé, Kane, kisses me on the head as he goes off to his job. I then slowly fall back asleep until I choose, because I'm on my own alarm clock. Now, most Gen Y's are night owls who will stay up all night and love a sleep in. I'm one of them. As I wake mid-morning, I sit up in bed and meditate to keep my body and mind at peace and gain gratitude to create an abundant-filled day. Then, as if I've slept with a coat hanger in my mouth, I beam the biggest grin and bounce out of bed to get ready for my exercises. I'll then either go off for a run, bike ride, or even boxing. Whilst nourishing my body, I love to feed my mind and my soul as well, so I listen to podcasts or audio books rather than the twenty-first century *bangers*. Once I've finished, I feel pumped and ready to create an abundant-filled day.

I then travel to my 'office.' It may be by the beach in Noosa while having a glass of wine in a chilled restraint, or in my local favourite health food shop having a juice, or on a picnic blanket by the lake. Maybe under my Doona cover keeping warm in winter.

Then I do my mentoring and coaching with the leadership in my organisation over Skype or Zoom, from anywhere in Australia and in the world where I allow the space for greatness and success to grow. I will then get in my brand-new white Mercedes and drive to the city to meet with a potential business partner who's becoming a part of my network and a Gen Y boss. I share the value of how much network marketing has impacted my life and my family's life, and paint the picture and vision for an everyday person living an extraordinary life.

How do you stay motivated in your business, and how do you motivate others to stay motivated?

To be motivated, and to give motivation, is such a funny thing, because to me it just feels as if it's temporary. Like, why can't we be inspired every day? In network marketing and in business, everything is a choice. Sometimes we don't like to admit it, but we've made choices to create what our reality looks like and what our business looks like right now. Never have I been 'motivated.' I wake up every day with the muscle and a habit to feel the vision and feel the message.

In everything I do, whether it's a training, a business meeting, or a coaching session, it has to be FUN and has to excite me and light up my body, because in today's society we're conditioned to believe that fun and business can't be in the same sentence. But when I say the word entrepreneur, you feel that fun. I love to wake up and do the things that are the most fun and creative for me, whether that's colouring in, going on adventures, exploring, or even exercising.

Something I've always believed is that when you become aware of what your message is to this world and become moved by your message, there's no way your message won't move others. It all has to start with you. If you're not inspired by your own vision, how do you expect anyone else to be? If you're moved by the work you do, then success and money is just an afterthought and a by-product of what you're creating and allowing into your life daily.

One of my favourite quotes is by Joan of Arc. "I am not afraid...I was born to do this." Her quote sums up my journey so perfectly, as I became not afraid to get out into the world to share my message and that burning ROAR inside of me. I wanted to share everything I knew and everything I believed in. I had a big vision to create a movement in this world for something different and unique for other Gen Y bosses to share their *roar*. Don't wait around for your team to be motivated or for you to be inspired. Be inspired by your own message and your own vision, and just go out there and show up in the world. Follow your roar and make it louder than any other noises in your head. Then you won't ever have to worry about being "motivated" again.

What do you believe is the main reason you've succeeded in this industry when others haven't?

I truly believe in my heart that anyone can build success in this industry, but it's not for everyone. There are numerous parts I believe have made up my puzzle of success.

In the twenty-first century, competition is an old model. For our generation we believe in co-petition, in which our unity is where our strength lies. In network marketing, this is a fundamental part of our business. We rise by teaching others how to build wealth, success, and freedom. There's no room for competition, judgment or wrongness. Now more than ever, we need to rise up and become more.

Every day, with every choice I make and every piece that's created, there's a trust and a knowing of my own intuition. My intuition knows me better than anyone. It knows my vision better than I do, so whenever I create and function, it comes from trust of my intuition. Traditionally in today's society, we're taught and conditioned from the moment we walk into the first day of primary school to become a rational decision- maker. However, in the last decade there's been a movement where organisational leaders and entrepreneurs are breaking free from those chains and are beginning to acknowledge the value of intuition. This allows us Generation Y bosses to become forward thinkers, future leaders, and visionaries.

Twenty-somethings will join this business and are set up to fail straight away. They have this bizarre relationship with 'goals' that aren't even theirs. They'll set a goal as to what they believe they *should* have in their life rather than what they *feel* is right for them. I've been at both ends of the spectrum. I came into this industry and set goals, but now I only set targets that are a personal guidance as to what I feel is light and expansive for me and will contribute to the world. When I do my morning meditation, I don't picture what my goal looks like. I don't say my goal twenty times over. I feel the way it would feel to have achieved and created that target. Then when an obstacle trips me up, I know it isn't a block or something holding me back. Instead it's a test to see if I I'm capable of creating my vision.

I see it time and time again in this industry, and I personally did this over and over again. I wasn't in true alignment with what I wanted to do and instead concentrated on what I thought I should do. When you make choices in your everyday business, you're going against yourself by setting a target that isn't true for you. Your soul doesn't want to get there, and neither do you. Goals and targets are meant to be our best friend when they're enjoyable, fun, and happy. Own your goals and honour them. You only deserve to have an amazing relationship with them, as they are the creation of your future.

What are the daily tasks essential to your network marketing business?

In a professional network marketing business, you need to become three things: a creator, a connector, and a mover. So within my days and the pockets of time I have, this is how I choose to implement them.

1. Becoming the connector.

    In my path every day, I'm searching for people who were me three years ago and who are looking to create a movement within their world, even if they don't know it yet. I'm always building relationships, friendships, and connecting with people I've known for fifteen years or fifteen minutes. There will always be someone turning eighteen, someone retiring, and someone losing their job, and they require different possibilities. This has been a fundamental skill in my business, especially when starting with no network

2. Becoming the creator.

    Coaching and mentoring is a fundamental part of the network marketing industry. Being the only CEO in your company is aging, and I LOVE that. We're conditioned by our teachers, family, friends, and uneducated people who will happily give you their advice or opinions that you must work on your weaknesses and strengthen them.

    But as young entrepreneurs, we see the business world from a whole other perspective. We focus a hundred percent on our best skills and strengths. We then learn how to surround ourselves with people who complement our weaknesses. We are the creation of our own businesses and our own leadership, so acknowledging who we are and what we become is how the young millionaires and billionaires are creating the world.

3. Becoming the mover.

    People are watching and trends are growing on this planet around young entrepreneurs who have a purpose and a sense of urgency in their life. One day I woke up and became aware how much *now* matters and that *someday* is killing so many dreams.

    Becoming the mover is all about becoming unapologetically you and not allowing others' thoughts, opinions, and emotions to paralyse and stump where you're going. When you pursue greatness, don't expect others to support you, because you will represent the courage, strength, boldness, and vision they don't have yet.

Shannon L. Alder said, "Confidence is knowing who you are and not changing it a bit because of someone's version of your reality is not their reality". I challenge you to become fearless in everything you do. Have an unshakeable and unwavering belief in who you're becoming and what you're creating as you take risks and live spontaneously in a world full of possibilities.

What does your future look like now, because of this opportunity?

Mark Twain said, "The two most important days in your life are the day you are born, and the day you find out why." Over the last three years, I've definitely found my passion and my purpose as to why I was put on this earth twenty-two years ago. My future looks completely the opposite of what it could have been. I could be slaving away working forty-sixty hours a week paying someone else's mortgage and wishing away five amazing days of the week just to enjoy two of them.

Our life is our own experiment, and I wake up every day to go on my very own adventure. I'm a spontaneous person, so I love doing this from the place of excitement and what is the most fun for me. I have the choice now to live a life by design, which means I can live anywhere in the world, doing whatever I want, whenever I would love to do it. I truly believe that that we, as leaders of our generation, have found a better way and want the same for those who are willing to stand out from the crowd, create something amazing, and make a lasting impact on their world.

Thanks to network marketing, we have the ability to live a bolder, grander, and brighter life. To live what we're born to do, which is choose happiness and freedom in every way we can imagine.

I'm now twenty two, and I created a list when I was twenty that was called *25 Before 25*. This was a list of twenty-five achievements I wanted to accomplish by the time that I turn 25. This business and industry has allowed me to stop playing small and dream bigger than I ever gave myself the opportunity to. I encourage you to write your list of *20 before 20* or *16 things to do in 2016*. Feel it, believe it, and DO IT.

Here is my list of *25 before 25* that will give you a flash into my future

1. Move to a tropical place in Australia

2. Ride in a hot air balloon in Barossa Valley SA

3. Have a *Never Say No* New York trip

4. Build a tree house

5. Create my own fashion line/charity

6. Swim with the dolphins

7. Read twenty leadership/business books

8. Jump the wake on my wakeboard

9. Give free hugs

10. Become a clean eater

11. Bungee jump in New Zealand

12. Create a domino effect of random acts of kindness

13. Bring my beautiful fiancé, Kane, home to fulfil his dream of restoring old cars

14. Spoil my family

15. Get married by the water

16. Pick flowers in my favourite peony field

17. Learn how to run 5 ks

18. Purchase my first piece of land

19. Road trip with my badass best friends

20. Earn more to give more

21. Ride a camel

22. Scuba dive on the Great Barrier Reef

23. Become a seven-figure earner

24. Learn Mandarin

25. Watch the sunset in ten different countries and cities

What are your top five tips for an aspiring Gen Y to succeed in network marketing?

1. YOUR VIBE ATTRACTS YOUR TRIBE.

    Behind every young millionaire, billionaire, and entrepreneur, you will find a wise mentor that will guide them, challenge them, and focus them on thinking bigger. Success rises and falls with the network you surround yourself with. You may or may not start off with a fantastic network that matches your vision, but what excites me about that is that you're about to learn an amazing skill and tool within your business in regard to networking.

    If you want to have greatness in your life, surround yourself with great people. Jim Rohn says, "You are the average of the five people you spend most time with." You are a product of who you surround yourself with, so be conscious who you allow into your circle. As a twenty-two year old, I had learnt a lot of lessons in business but knew I had a lot more to learn. I was growing strength to strength and working out what kind of leader I wanted to become. I surrounded myself with likeminded people who were going in the same direction, and I was inspired by and moved by. I became friends with them and treated them as an equal, and slowly but surely I started to mirror their characteristics and success, whilst still being me. I loved the message they were sharing with the world. I will always remember this saying that made me conscious of who I spent my time with: "Never believe someone else's opinion if you wouldn't trade lives with them."

2. BECOME HUNGRY.

Every year for thirteen years in school, I hated learning. I was extremely creative, but when it came to academics I would be walking out of the class with a detention. As soon as I began my journey in entrepreneurship as a Gen Y boss, I had a thirst for knowledge and to create more in the world. Every car trip I would learn from the best. Every training or networking event I went to, I had a real hunger to create a movement. Until you have that burning hunger and willingness to choose something different in your life and in your network marketing business, you'll just dabble along slowly, and that's what I did until one day when I took off my rose-coloured ***glasses and saw the true, authentic beauty of what this industry is.

3. CAN YOU SPOT THE CHAMELEON LEADER?

Twenty-somethings don't have many life experiences under their belt. I know I didn't. All I knew was how to make a good coffee and a sandwich. But when I had to step into a multibillion-dollar industry and coach and mentor people who were thirty-forty years ahead of me, I learned to become the chameleon leader.

What this meant was adapting to different networks with different backgrounds and different age groups. Having the willingness to look at life from other perspectives and what I would do differently. Think about your business. If you're forty five and have two kids, are you limiting yourself by not tapping into the Gen Y market being a part of your business? That doesn't mean you have to be sixty and going out clubbing, it just means you have the willingness to see business and network marketing from their point of view. And if you're twenty four and love going out and partying with your other twenty-something friends, you're not tapping into Gen X and baby boomers.

4. BE YOUR MESSAGE.

As I say, the being is more powerful than the actual doing, and in this case, it's absolutely true. It took me some time after getting into my business and growing up to realise what my burning message was. I believe it's our responsibility to share our message with the world. Learn how to release your fears, be unapologetically you, and share your voice with pride.

Network marketing is your vehicle to share your message with the world. If it's to bring more mums home to their babies or like me, to create a movement of Gen Y's to contribute to the world in more ways than what we're conditioned to.

Allow your message to be so unapologetically real and raw, that it just bleeds through you with every Instagram post, every connection you make, or even any time you're in someone's presence. This is the being rather than the doing of your message. You need to trust and know that as you share your message with the world, more will be received. When you deliver it from a place of inspiration and love, that's exactly how it will be received in the world. It will create a dynamic movement of something so unique that it will shift the everyday grind. It's our time to shake up this earth and say there's more.

5. BE THE ONE WHO GOES FIRST

When I first joined my incredible network marketing business three years ago, there weren't any younger Gen Y leaders I could aspire to be like, so I knew in my heart I had to become the one who goes first. Even when I had the world's best mentors, I didn't really have anyone the same age who'd paved the way.

You may be the first person in your family, or friends, or in your whole entire town, to choose something different. Believe in that with every inch of your body, because there will be someone like you waiting for you to become that invitation of inspiration to create more in their future. Embrace being the entrepreneur and being called the positive one or the weird one. Be the one who's freaked out by the normal and the misunderstood ones. Little do you know that you're the courageous one to go first and create a movement for MORE. This life was meant to be courageously lived and to sprinkle your joy, kindness, and magic everywhere. Why hold that back from the world?

CHAPTER 8

Dr Jacqui Way

"*You become what you believe. You are where you are today in your life based on everything you have believed.*"

Oprah Winfrey

CHAPTER EIGHT

Dr Jacqui Way

What is your background?

While growing up on a property in rural Victoria, my dream was to become a veterinarian, so I could heal animals and provide animal husbandry for farmers and rural communities. I lived in a modest weatherboard home with my parents, grandfather, and younger brother. Together we bred and showed stud beef cattle. This became a passion of mine that inspired me during my teenage years and led me on the path to becoming a veterinary surgeon.

My parents are both nurses and established their own aged care facility shortly after completing their education and intensive training in a Melbourne hospital. My parents had a vision for themselves and their family and created a phenomenal business from the ground up. My dad believed that this was the only way he could be a male nurse and be his own boss. I grew up watching and admiring them both. They inspired me from a young age with their vision, their hard work, and they had the determination to create more for their family.

I wasn't academically inclined at school, and I vividly remember meeting with the careers teacher prior to commencing my VCE and sharing with him my hopes and dreams to study at the University of Melbourne's Veterinary Science School. His response was one of those moments in life where you know deep down no one will ever stop you. He explained to me that I was only a B-grade student, and these dreams of mine were just that. Dreams. He said I should start looking at other VCE subject choices and career paths. I was encouraged to study Economics, but I refused to drop any of the prerequisite subjects for Veterinary Science. I was determined to become what I believed I could be, even if no one else could see that life for me. Something inside of me knew that I could do anything I believed and I had the internal drive to create that, even when others doubted my abilities and told me otherwise.

At the end of Year 12 I didn't have the grades required for admission into Veterinary Science, so I started studying Agricultural Economics in Sydney.

I knew this wasn't for me, so after one year I returned to Melbourne to study science, with the aim of completing first year and gaining a place in Veterinary Science. After a year of solid study while working part-time as a veterinary nurse, I applied for Veterinary Science. After an interview with the dean, he offered me a position in the course the following year. All of my dreams had come true. My year of hard work and focused study had paid off. When I graduated as a veterinary surgeon, I applied for my first job in a small rural town in NSW.

It was here I met my husband to be, over the backend of a cow as he helped me to replace a uterine prolapse. We fell madly in love quickly, and we were both ready for a change. So when an opportunity to relocate was offered, we decided to move our family back to Victoria and bought a gorgeous little property on the edge of town.

I was now a mother to two young girls and a fulltime veterinarian. It was almost immediately apparent that my work-family balance wasn't compatible for me. We knew we wanted more babies, but I couldn't be the wife and mother I wanted to be. I felt trapped. I didn't know what other options I had. We'd become accustomed to the lifestyle my income provided for our family and didn't think there were any other options.

I enjoyed educating others and inspiring them to become the best version of themselves, so I also followed this passion as a lecturer for senior veterinary nurses studying Diploma of Veterinary Nursing. This led me down the path of returning to university myself and completing postgraduate studies in Education. I graduated from this degree with four kids and pregnant with my fifth. However, I still wasn't completely fulfilled, I love inspiring others in this way, but I was still feeling lost, trapped, and uninspired. The work-family balance was still not where I desired it to be. I was sacrificing a lot working, studying, and being a mum. I wanted a beautifully balanced life but had no idea how to create it. I knew they was more out there, and I was open to the possibilities and opportunities.

How did you get into network marketing?

My neighbour had a network marketing business that she did alongside numerous other business pursuits. I knew how much it made her happy, because I could see the way she would light up when talking about it. I'd always been intrigued about how these types of businesses worked. How could successful, professional women leave there secure six-figure jobs for these businesses?

I was invited me to watch a presentation presented by my future upline, Debbie Loughnane, and she painted the picture for me. For the first time in a long time, I started to dream again. She spoke with energy and lightness that drew me in. I was so inspired by her, even though we'd never met. I started to create a vision for my family and how this business could create exactly what I was longing for personally, professionally, and financially. I knew before the presentation was finished that I was going to give this a go, because I couldn't see a reason not to, and I believed that this opportunity would create the beautifully balance life I'd been searching for. I saw very little risk in jumping straight in, especially with the low setup costs associated with a network marketing business versus traditional business.

In my case, opening my own veterinary practice, or buying into one, was no comparison. I was scared that if I kept doing what I was doing, I'd keep getting what I was getting, and I was unhappy in my current situation and wanted to create another life for myself, my husband, and our children.

So two weeks before baby number five was born, I launched my business, spent a week in hospital recovering from a caesarean section, and got promoted to district manager as my baby turned four weeks old. I had a crystal-clear vision to create a beautifully balanced life. I would own my time and be able to stay home with my children when I wanted without it affecting my income. That's why I jumped straight into it. I had very little to lose with the minimal setup costs. It was just a matter of sharing the products I loved and the opportunity to change people's lives.

My first year in the business I experienced a lot of personal growth. I built a consistently strong, sustainable group of clients, as well as my team. I continued to duplicate the system created by my upline leaders and promoted my first district manager, who was also my sister in law. Within the next six months, our organisation was in tremendous momentum, and all of the business I'd been building resulted in us becoming our own region. This was the catalyst for my team, and together we've continued to build and grow and have so much fun creating the life we choose.

What is your vision for your business?

My vision is to change the lives of other women who felt like I did prior to learning about network marketing. Showing them there's another possibility to have a beautifully balanced life and be in control of their time, whilst creating wealth. This is what motivates me and continues to inspire me to share the opportunity with others.

In just a couple of years running my own network marketing business, my entire outlook on life has changed. I'm enjoying each day that I have at home with my family and own my time again. I'm also travelling. I'd forgotten how much I loved these experiences. I truly thought travel was so far removed from my reality that I didn't even dream about it. My five children all have passports now, as we've been given the gift of overseas five-star holidays. These holidays have given us a chance to create unforgettable memories together, something that was never possible prior to this business.

My husband and I have experienced travelling together overseas and now plan at least one holiday together every year. I thought this was something we'd only get to experience once our children had grown up, and I'd been worried we'd be too old to enjoy it. Because of these experiences for myself personally and with my family, I'm fulfilled in ways I never knew existed. I'm so grateful I was open to the opportunity to take a look at something completely different to the reality I was living. The most exciting part is that it's only the beginning, and I know there's so much more out there available to me. My vision is growing daily, and I'm excited to reach out and make it my reality.

Who has inspired and influenced you, and why?

I've had many people who inspire and influence me, including both of my parents, my grandfather, my husband, and my upline, Debbie Loughnane.

My mum has inspired me to be the best mother I can be to my children. She's always put my brother and me first and values family. She still inspires and guides me every day and has believed and supported me throughout my life. For that I'm forever grateful to her. I love the relationship she's created with her grandchildren and how much they love and adore her.

My dad is a true entrepreneur and inspires me every day with what he's created in his lifetime for himself and our family. He saw an opportunity early in his career to create the business and lifestyle of his dreams and has built it into an incredible organisation. His business success continues to grow as he enjoys both time and financial freedom.

My grandfather lived with me most of my childhood and was a big influence on my life and the person I've become. He was a strong, hardworking, genuine man who I admired. He inspired me to follow my dreams and never give up.

Since starting my network marketing business, my upline leader, Debbie, has been my biggest influence. She empowered me to believe in me again, find my awareness, and inspired me to create a phenomenal organisation. I desire to become a leader like her and duplicate her success with my organisation.

What do you find are the main differences between being a vet and running a network marketing business?

They are remotely opposite. By running my own network marketing business, I own my time and set my flexible working hours around my family. I can work anywhere as long as I have a computer and phone and the ability to leverage my time.

When I was working as a vet, my time and hours were dictated by my boss and a list of scheduled consultations and emergencies. Being on call was the trickiest for me to manage as a mum, especially with my husband's busy and unpredictable schedule. The hardest part was that I couldn't even guarantee I'd be at the bus stop to pick up my kids, and if I was out on a farm with a large animal emergency, often I didn't know what the time was, because my phone was out of range.

I felt helpless, and living in a new town meant I didn't have anyone else to rely on to take care of my children. Being on call often meant I'd miss family events and not be available when my kids needed me, so it just made our life unpredictable. I could never be relied upon. I love that I'm now in a hundred percent control of my day and how I schedule my business. I know my priorities and fill my calendar with them first. Then my business fits into the spaces available. For me, my children, and my husband, this makes our life beautifully balanced.

You're a busy mum of five kids. How do you manage to rotate you business around your life, and what advice do you have for busy mums?

As a mother of five, I believe organisation is vital to the sustainability and success of my business and allows me to have the balance that makes me and my family happy. I'm going to share with you a few techniques I used to help me create the life I love with my business.

1. Know your priorities

   What are you really prioritising? Are they your priorities or someone else's? Write them down and look at them every day. That will help you to decide what and when you need to get things done. For example, knowing my priorities helps me to allocate my week and schedule my calendar.

2. Make to-do lists each day and tick them off as you go.

   Carry over the tasks you don't get done. This helps me to not have too much in my mind, so it's not sent into overdrive. I make lists for everything, using my phone, sticky notes, or on paper. Lists prevent me from getting overwhelmed and flustered when I have lots of activities on the go at once. I refer back to my priorities to decide what needs to be completed first.

3. Outsource where possible.

   I've found outsourcing amazing. I can achieve much more when I'm not overwhelmed. Think about what you don't like to do and always put off. Can you outsource these chores? For me it was ironing and cleaning bathrooms. The other point to consider when outsourcing is knowing the value of your time. My dad taught me to think this way. There are tasks that only you can do, and you need to do them. Then there are tasks other people can do for you that will free up your time.

Maybe there are tasks that will be done more efficiently and effectively if you outsource them. For a lot of mums, it's hard to let go at the start, because we often want to do everything and do it our way, but what if you could let go of that thought? Think about how much more you could achieve. What difference would that make in your business?

Outsourcing doesn't always need to cost you money. Using the barter system can work. All it takes is some creative thinking and simply asking the person you're exchanging with what would be possible. I've used it for numerous goods and services in my life.

4.   Take time out for you.

I include time out for myself and exercise as two of my priorities. I make time for them every day by simply allocating it in my daily planner. Consistently creating this time for yourself is vital and has made a significant difference in my world.

5.   Communication with my husband.

We have five children with a large age range, from senior secondary school to nappies, and we both run our own businesses, so it's fair to say we have a lot going on. At times when our communication is minimal, we become stressed and issues appear worse than they really are.

Communication is vital to our family's wellbeing and our business success. I value that we know each other's schedules and each other's goals, dreams, and desires. Since I started my business, we often talk about our yearly, five year, ten year, and retirement plan. Before we just lived for each day and never through too far into the future. This type of forward-thinking communication has created a common target we know together we're working towards to create a life we love.

How has this industry changed your life? Do you think about what your life would have looked like without this opportunity?

The network marketing industry has completely changed my life. It's breathed life back into me. I now dream again, and those dreams become realities. I have visions of my, and my family's, future. These visions excite me and keep me motivated to drive my business forward.

The industry also involves a lot of personal development, and this is something I'd never experienced in my profession as a veterinary surgeon. I've grown so much and evolved into a much more confident person who knows who she is and is completely comfortable with herself. There was a time in my life when I did lose the sense of who I was and started to become someone else, but this business, and the personal development I've done, has helped me to find the true me again.

It's funny to think about what my life would have looked like without this opportunity, because I've learnt so much about myself. It's almost like I didn't even know I was missing out on anything. But honestly, I think I would have become more unhappy as the years passed, because I felt trapped. I would have stopped loving what I was doing and started resenting it every day, which would have been a sad way to live. And what makes me feel the saddest is thinking about what my kids would have thought of me. Would I have inspired them? Would they want to be like me? I now know that you become what you believe, and I'm where I am today based on everything I've believed.

What has been the biggest hurdle you've overcome to get to where you are, and how did you overcome it?

Throughout the journey of my business there have been numerous blockers that have appeared along the way. Sometimes I've been able to identity and deal with them immediately, and at other times it's taken a while to gain awareness of them. The key is to be open and ask questions of yourself when you're feeling like you aren't moving forward. Be aware. When we aren't in awareness, our ability to move forward is hindered and can slow us down. Then we need to be willing to accept this awareness and work through a solution to overcome it.

I see this in others people's businesses. Often that they're aware but aren't willing to find the solutions. These people are self-sabotaging themselves and their business, and to some degree we all do it from time to time. But when we're in awareness, we can receive the solutions we need. Having an open and honest relationship with your upline leader is vital to overcoming hurdles in your business. Your upline leaders have experienced similar situations to the ones you're going through and often know where to go for the help that's needed.

If you were able to go back and start again, what would you do differently?

I wouldn't change anything. I don't have any regrets. Hindsight is valuable, but I'd rather learn from my experiences, so I can gain awareness and use what I learned to move forward. I don't dwell on what's happened in the past, as I know I can't go back in time. I'm grateful for my experiences. They've helped shape me as a leader for my organisation, and I pass on what I've learnt, so my team doesn't have to make the same mistakes or reinvent the wheel.

My years in network marketing have helped me grow as a person, and this journey had to take time. I had to have certain experiences. Without those experiences, I would have never learnt. Our experiences make us stronger, and if we're willing to be aware and learn from them, they will shape the future.

How do you stay motivated, and how do you motivate others?

I stay motivated in my business, because of my vision of where I'm going. My family's future also motivates me. I continue to want to create more for my family. I can't motivate others. I can only inspire and empower them to follow their dreams as I do. I encourage everyone in my organisation to always know their *why*, as it can change over time. It's essential to their business that they know why they're doing what they're doing. I recommend writing your *why* down and placing it somewhere that you look every day, to remind you why you've chosen to create your business. Know what your vision is for the next three, six, or twelve months. What are your targets, and what do you want to achieve?

My vision is to inspire and empower other people to have the same life balance I've been able to achieve with my business. I'm passionate about sharing with everyone who's looking for that same balance, because I know it can completely change their life if they believe it can. Every person who launches their business for the first time motivates me. I get so excited when I know I can empower them to create something more for themselves and their families.

What are the three ways you've built your resilience to people saying no and having judgments about this industry?

The way I've built my resilience to judgments about the industry is based on my belief system.

1. BELIEF IN MYSELF.

    I believe I'm an example to others who are looking to create a better work-life balance for themselves, because I know I've achieved it, and I'm extremely passionate to share my experiences with anyone who is open.

2. BELIEF IN MY PRODUCTS.

    I know the products are exactly what they claim to be, and I believe in the transparency in the ingredient policy of my company.

3. BELIEF IN MY OPPORTUNITY.

    I'm so grateful to share this opportunity. I know it can change anyone's life if they're willing to create those changes. I don't take anyone else's point of view personally, because they're often uneducated views or they're not open to the possibility of something a bit different than what they're used to. I'm aware that the industry isn't for everyone, and if we all did the same thing, wouldn't life be pretty boring?

    As my belief grew in myself, the products, and the opportunity, so did my resilience to other people's conclusions and judgments.

Would you give your top five tips for success in network marketing?

My five tips for success in network marketing are:

1. BELIEVE IN YOURSELF, THE PRODUCTS, AND THE OPPORTUNITY.

   It's paramount to your success in network marketing, as this is a belly-to-belly business, and if your belief isn't a hundred percent in all of these areas, people will see straight through you and not listen to anything you have to share with them.

2. BE DUPLICABLE.

   You are the ripple effect, and everything you do will be duplicated by the people who join you. The fastest way to grow is to duplicate a proven system of success, follow your upline's advice, and do what has been proven by others to be successful, so you will also have success.

3. BE THE BEST VERSION OF YOURSELF.

   Be the best version of you and the number one leader in your organisation. Lead from the front and by example, and people will choose to follow in your successful footsteps and create what you're creating. You start the ripple effect and control how wide it flows out. Think about that when you have a major decision to make.

4. BE CONSISTENT.

   No matter what system you choose to follow, you must follow it consistently. If you choose to create success in your network marketing business, you can't just turn it on and off. You need to continue with a consistent level of activity, always. My promotions to higher management levels came over twelve months into my business, but I had continued to consistently be in activity. That's why I have the business I do now. Because I built the strong foundations from the start, it has allowed my business to continue to grow and flourish.

5. BE COACHABLE.

Listen to and respect your upline. They only want success for you and can share with you what worked and didn't work for them. There's no need to reinvent the wheel or make the same mistakes, so listen to them and be grateful for their words of wisdom. If you want to create their success for yourself, then they are the best mentor you can ever have.

CHAPTER 9

Kaitlyn Cummins

"You get in life what you have the courage to ask for."

Oprah Winfrey

CHAPTER NINE

Kaitlyn Cummins

What is your background?

I grew up in a small country town of three-hundred people. I was the oldest of four children, and our life was pretty standard. Both of my parents worked hard to give us every opportunity, and we had a wonderful childhood. Dad was a harvesting contractor. Like many self-employed people, he worked long hours and weekends, and during harvest he would have to work away for months at a time.

Through those early years, my mum was a nurse. She worked nights to save on childcare costs and to be home with us kids during the day. In her spare time she worked as a seamstress making dresses for local women, and on weekends she worked in a little railway carriage in town that she and some friends had turned into a homemade giftware shop.

When I was ten, she finally got to quit her nursing job, which she hated, and she started her own florist and gift shop. Whilst she had found a career she enjoyed, she worked fifty to sixty hours per week. With four young children to run around after and a husband who was rarely home, her life was busy.

My parents were forty before they went on their first big holiday together, which was two weeks in Broome. It was my dad's first time on an airplane, and they had an amazing time. They came home with the travel bug and booked another holiday for the following year. However, a few months after they got home from that first trip, mum was diagnosed with cancer. We were devastated. Our local school only went to year ten, so I was away at boarding school when we got the news. The months that followed were a blur of hospital stays, surgeries, radiation therapy, trial studies, and countless hours in the car travelling for treatment. Mum was too unwell to go on that second holiday they'd booked. Fourteen months after being diagnosed, she passed away at age forty one.

I was only seventeen when my mum died. I had just finished year 12, and the day of her funeral was when first-round university offers came out. I remember someone coming up to me at her funeral and saying, "Congratulations!" I thought they were crazy, but that was how I found out I'd been accepted into the Bachelor of Health Science, Occupational Therapy course. My initial reaction was, "Nope, not this year. It starts in four weeks. I can't do it." The thought of packing up again, moving away from home, and starting something as big as this was scary and completely overwhelming. Then, right there in the local football clubrooms, surrounded by seven-hundred mourners, I weighed up my options. I could curl up at home and hide, or I could live my life the way my parents never got to live theirs.

From that moment on, I set about saying YES to every opportunity that presented itself. If my life was going to be as short as mum's, I didn't want it to be as stressful, tiring, busy, and full of hard work as my parents' lives were. I wanted to travel, have fun, feel relaxed, and enjoy each day. So over the next few years, whilst studying and working as a cleaner at our local golf club, I did lots of travelling. I went to cheap places at first, like Bali, Thailand, Malaysia, and then a summer holiday working and skiing in Vail in Colorado. I used my placements as opportunities to travel as well, and went to Queensland, Sydney, Melbourne, and Outback NSW.

After finishing university, I packed up my car and drove across the Nullarbor to Perth, where I lived and worked for two years in a private psychiatric hospital. In 2008 I came home for what was to be a short visit before moving to Canada to work. The day I arrived home, I ran into an old friend from school. He was home on holidays. I was surprised how excited I was to see him and how much we enjoyed each other's company. Within a few weeks my plans had changed. I started working locally, saved some money, and built a house. I still had the travel bug, so we did some short trips to Europe, Langkawi, and Vanuatu before getting married and starting our family.

What were some of your early jobs?

I loved helping people, and in my job as an occupational therapist, I got to work with children and their families. It was so rewarding. At uni, my best friend Sarah and I always joked about how we would marry someone wealthy and only work part time once we graduated. We soon realized we hadn't fallen in love with millionaires, and we needed more than a part-time income to support our lifestyles. I always felt so constrained by the four weeks of leave I would get each year, since it didn't allow me the freedom to do what I had planned.

That's when I decided to start a private practice in occupational therapy. I thought working for myself would change all of that. It certainly gave me flexibility, but in a fee-for-service industry like OT, if you're not working, you don't get paid. Again, this just didn't fit with my goals to have freedom, flexibility, and choices. My goal was to relax and enjoy each day and to not have to worry about money.

How did you get into network marketing?

At twenty eight, I got married. My husband and I had good jobs, a solid income, and a nice lifestyle, but there wasn't enough money left after we paid our bills for us to travel, and we certainly would not be able to live comfortably on one income. I was looking for something else. We had dabbled in property investing and the stock market, but without money to invest, our options were limited.

Then my friend asked me to take a look at a business she'd started. She was home on maternity leave at the time, and I assumed she'd started a party plan to give her a bit of extra income. I had just started in a management position at our local hospital and was still juggling my private practice. The last thing I thought I needed was a little party plan business, and I hated going to them, so the thought of starting one myself made me laugh. Except for one thing. It had been eleven years since my mum died, and I held strong to the decision I'd made at her funeral that if an opportunity presented itself, I would always consider it. This habit of saying yes had guided me well to this point, so I agreed to take a look.

What had my attention was the business model. It was exactly the opportunity I'd been looking for, however it was the last place I thought I would find it. It was an opportunity to help others, to build an asset, to leverage my time, and to do it alongside my other commitments. What was better was that it was something I was already spending money on, which was a consumable range of products everyone already used. It was just a matter of redirecting my spending, which allowed me to turn an expense into an income, and show others how they could do the same. The next day I signed up, purchased my kit, and set about learning everything I could about the company, the products, and the network marketing industry.

What are your three favourite things about network marketing?

I love that this business allows me to be smart with my time, to do the work once, and be paid for it over and over again. Not only that, but when I teach and train others how to do what I do, I get the benefits of time leverage. In occupational therapy, if you work forty hours a week, you only get paid for those forty hours. In network marketing, I work on average ten hours per week, and I teach and train others how to do that as well. If I teach one other person who also works ten hours, then I get paid on my ten plus their ten, and so on. It gets really exciting when those people teach others.

My husband, Marcus, is a school teacher. In his industry it doesn't matter how hard you work, how good you are at your job, or how many hours you put in, you get paid on years of experience, so his earning potential is limited. I love that in network marketing, you get paid on effort. If you work hard, take time to become good at what you do, and put in the hours, you get paid accordingly. At the start it generally feels like a lot of effort for not a lot of reward, but with consistency, you quickly notice the shift of less time, more reward. Over time you start to see your efforts compounding, and those initial thoughts of wondering, *Is this worth it?* becomes, *Wow, am I worth this much?* It's incredible.

In traditional business when you retire, your income stops. You can work for forty years and retire with nothing tangible to show for it. I love that in network marketing, you're not trading time for money. You're building an asset that will pay you well after you retire, and continue to pay your family if anything ever happens to you. Networking marketing is by far the smartest business model I've seen, and I urge anyone who's looking for a change to educate themselves on how this industry actually works.

How is network marketing different and more attractive than being in the healthcare industry?

A few weeks ago I paid my OT registration, something I still do and will continue to do, because I'm proud of the twelve years I've served in the industry, and I enjoy being able to work with the children at our local primary and special development schools. My registration fee includes my OT membership and insurances, and costs me over $1,000 each year. This is in addition to the $30,000 my degree cost and the expense of supporting myself through four years of study, long placements, and twenty hours of professional development each year.

My network marketing business costs me $110 per year. I've been able to earn an income from day one, even while I was learning the business, and after eighteen months with the company, working an average of ten hours per week, I had replaced my fulltime occupational therapy income that had taken forty hours per week and ten years for me to reach. When I look at young people graduating university now with all of these expenses and limited job opportunities in their chosen field, I can't help but wonder why society keeps encouraging young people to take this path. It doesn't lead to job certainty and certainly not job security. Nor does it equal financial freedom. My husband is thirty years old, he went to university straight out of school, and only this month has he made his final HECS payments. That's four years of studying, followed by eight years he spent paying for it.

In network marketing, rather than being paid for the hours you work, you get paid for the value you add. I love that the work you do now can continue to reward you for years to come. In healthcare, if you did a great job, showed creativity, efficiency, or that you had a skill in a specific area, you were given more work, more expectations, and less time to complete them. In network marketing not only are you paid for that first effort, but if you added value and educated or up-skilled others, you can be paid on that one effort infinitely, as the client you introduced continues to shop online and buy your product, or the consultant you up-skilled is able to help others.

Then there are the rewards. After ten years working in the health industry, the only extrinsic rewards I have to show for it are a 0.5% per annum pay rise and the occasional free lunch. In less than two years in network marketing, I've been rewarded with three amazing holidays all paid for by the company, Tiffany jewellery, a white Mercedes Benz, flowers for by birthday, Valentine's Day, Australia Day, Christmas presents every year, and an abundance of free personal and professional development.

When you started your network marketing business, what did you do to get it up and running?

I joined network marketing, because I was impressed with the business model and our company's compensation plan. I loved how simple, fair, and lucrative the opportunity was, and I could see the potential in this business straight away. However, I had no prior knowledge of the company, no experience with selling, no background in skincare, cosmetics or nutrition. Prior to starting my business I didn't wear makeup or know how to apply it, and my outfit of choice was tracksuit pants and a jumper. Shoes were not a necessity, and my ideal evening was sitting on the couch watching old episodes of *Friends*.

When the opportunity was presented to me, something in my gut told me I needed to give it a try. I said yes, signed up, and brought my kit. Then I didn't sleep for a week. The realisation of what I'd done occurred to me, and I knew that if I wanted to make this work, I needed to become an expert. I would not feel comfortable sharing our products or our opportunity with anyone, if I didn't have a rock-solid belief in the company, the products, and the industry.

I sat up till the early hours of the morning learning everything I could about network marketing, I read books, listened to audios, and Googled, Googled, and Googled some more. The more research I did the more my belief grew, and with that came this incredible excitement. For the first time in years, I felt hope that we could have everything we wanted in life, that I might not have to work a nine-to-five forever, that we could do everything and have everything we'd given up believing were possible, like owning our dream home, a nice car, a boat, and being able to travel whenever we wanted.

My life was really busy when I started my business. We were renovating our house, I was working full time, and I had just started a new senior position. I also had a private practice that I was trying to juggle, along with other commitments like playing and coaching the local netball team. I also sat on the board for the local football club. So in hindsight, I now know the business opportunity was just perfect for my situation. Because all of the learning is online, I was able to do it whenever I wanted. For me it was listening to audios and training instead of the music when I was driving, exercising, cleaning the house, or while my husband and I sat on the couch in the evenings. He would be watching TV and I would read, send emails, or watch online trainings on my laptop with the headphones on.

Who has inspired and influenced you, and why?

My parents have been a huge influence in my life and career. They taught me how to work hard, and for that I'm grateful. They also inspired me to want more. Watching my mum pass away at such a young age after spending more than twenty years working her butt off and not getting to enjoy the benefits of her years of effort, left me feeling determined to live the life she never could. It's been thirteen years now since she passed away, and I'm proud to look back and not feel regret. I've been able to build our dream life, without compromising my youth. I travel the world, spend time with my husband and our baby, and give back to my community. This is what brings me the most joy.

Once I started network marketing, I discovered the world of personal development. In the past two years I've read and listened to dozens of personal development stories, and they've absolutely shaped the life and success I've created during that time. Some of my biggest influences have included Robin Sharma's *5am project*, Dale Carnegie's *How to Win Friends and Influence People*, Napolean Hill's *Think and Grow Rich*, Oprah's *What I Know For Sure*, Jeff Olsen's *The Slight Edge*, and anything I can get my hands on by Tony Robbins.

I now commit thirty minutes each morning to listening to personal development while I exercise, and I read ten pages of a book each night before I go to bed. These, and so many other simple daily habits, are easy to do and are the reason my life has changed so drastically over the past two years. I encourage everyone to take the time to do this for themselves. When you apply these principles consistently over time, anything is possible. Try it and see for yourself.

If you were able to go back and start again, what would you do differently?

If I were able to start my business again, first, I would have started at eighteen, and I would also treat it like the multimillion dollar business it is. When I started I was excited about the opportunity, but I never gave the business, or myself, the respect we deserved. Whenever anyone asked me what I did for work, I would tell them I was an occupational therapist. For months I hid my business, for fear of what other people would think of me. I loved the products and would share them with some of my network, but I was selective with who I asked to try them and how I shared the opportunity.

Looking back now I think, "Who was I to judge like that?" Most people would never have assumed I would be interested in selling skincare and lipsticks, but imagine if they hadn't asked me because of that. What would my life look like now? The way I see it is that it's my job to share our products and the opportunity. The people I share it with get to decide if they want to try it or not. Now, I leave my judgment behind. I assume most people won't be interested, and that saves me the disappointment when they say no. But I tell them about it anyway, knowing that at least I gave them a choice.

How do you feel about your future, now that you've built a successful network marketing business?

When I started my business, I didn't have a lot of time to commit to it, so I took every opportunity I could get to listen to audio books and trainings. Then I applied what I learned straight away, so I moved through the management levels in our company relatively quickly. A few months after joining, I travelled to New York with my Aunty. We were visiting the Tiffany and Co store on 5th Avenue, and I had found a beautiful ring I wanted to purchase as a token of our trip. It was a seven-and-a-half carat quartz dress ring, and I just loved it. Of course it was not something I could afford at the time, so I put it on my bucket list in my mind, and we continued on our travels.

A few weeks later we attended our company's global training conference in Las Vegas, and I watched as these women were awarded on stage with beautiful Tiffany dress rings. I asked the lady in front of me what they had done to earn such an amazing award, and she explained that they were the twenty people worldwide who'd helped the most consultants promote to the first management level. I remember thinking for a split second, *I could do that. I would love one of those rings.* Then I never thought of it again.

Later that year I was in the Tiffany store on Collins St in Melbourne with a gift voucher I had received for coaching my local netball team. I saw the beautiful quartz ring, and even with my vouchers, I couldn't afford it, so I settled for the matching earrings, hoping that one day I would get the ring. Six months later I was invited to attend our global training conference in Las Vegas as an award recipient. Standing on stage in front of 18,000 people I opened my gift, and in the box was a beautiful quartz Tiffany dress ring the exact colour that matched my earrings and the exact size for my finger. I was one of twenty people who won that award, and everyone received a different ring. No one knew I wanted that particular ring, and it was at that moment I realised how powerful the universe is and that I had the potential to do something incredible with my life.

Every day I'm reminded of how powerful our thoughts are and the incredible manifestations we can create in our life when we ask for it. Network marketing has taught me to never limit my thinking. We have the power to create whatever life we choose. I'm two years into my network marketing career, and my life is completely unrecognisable. We live in our dream home, my husband has his dream speedboat, we drive a beautiful car paid for by our company, we take our family on incredible holidays, have more time to spend together, and more time to give back to our community, which is something that brings us both so much joy.

My husband, who was a big sceptic when I started, often says to me now that even without the money and the rewards, starting this business is the best decision I've ever made. He attributes the business, the company, the people I work alongside, and the learning I've done since I started, to making me a much happier, nicer, and more generous person.

I'm excited about the future that I'm creating for myself and my family. I'm excited about the impact we'll have on so many people in our local community and across the world through our company's opportunity. Also, through the time freedom I now have, I've been able to give back to projects

I'm passionate about. I know when I look back on my life twenty years from now, that's what I will be the most proud of. The impact I was able to have on the lives of others brings me joy, and that's what motivates me to keep growing and expanding my business.

What have been some of the rewards and recognitions you've achieved in your network marketing business?

In my first few months with the company I was awarded with a $100 spa voucher to use at our local day spa. I thought that was amazing, as I had never received an award at work before. But that was just the beginning of a string of incredible awards.

At my first Australian Company conference about twelve months into my business, I received an award onstage, for helping the most consultants promote to the first management level. I was completely taken by surprise. I'd been sitting at the back of the crowd of over two-thousand women. I was heavily pregnant and having one of those days when none of your clothes fit, and you feel more fat than pregnant. I was wearing thongs and a baggy t-shirt, hoping I would just blend into the background. You could imagine my embarrassment standing onstage in front of thousands of beautiful, well-dressed women. I learnt quickly not to under-dress at these events. Six months on, with a new baby by my side, I travelled to Las Vegas and was onstage again to receive the same award, this time on a global level.

In our short time in the business, my husband and I have earned two phenomenal five-star holidays to Fiji and Queensland with our family. On our most recent trip, we took our ten-month-old son and my husband's parents. They were just blown away by how incredible the experience was. We got to take them to Movie World and Dreamworld after hours, when the parks were closed to the public, and they were able to enjoy an abundance of free food and wine and go on the rides as many times as they wanted without lining up. It was just amazing. My husband, who was so nervous about going on the first one, has declared that we're never going to miss out on one of these trips. He loves them so much.

What has been the hardest moment in your business, and how did you overcome it? What advice do you have for anyone who may be experiencing hardship in their network marketing business or life?

The hardest part of my business was, and still is…. myself. That little voice in my head that tells me I'm not good enough, I don't know enough, that I'm not fit enough, friendly enough, or successful enough. There's a voice that says, I'm too tired or too busy, and there's one that tells me they won't be interested, they don't need this, they're too busy, or too successful. What if they say no? What if they laugh? Will they think I'm trying to sell them something? My solution is that I go back to working on myself.

The times when these thoughts take over are generally when my life is a bit chaotic and unstructured, so I go back to my simple daily disciplines. For me, getting over myself means getting the basics right. I do the physical activities I have choice and control over, like getting up early, exercising, eating well, reading ten pages of a book, meditating, making time for myself to do something I love, or taking thirty minutes each day to do some company-specific training. When the thoughts creep in again, and I start worrying about myself, I know I have it all wrong. This business is not about me. It's about what I can do for someone else, so I make sure when I'm speaking with someone that my focus is on how I can help them, what they need, and what's in it for them. When you take the focus off yourself and work towards helping as many other people as you can, then your success will take care of itself.

My other suggestion, for life and business is, *Don't quit!* The only way you fail in our industry is when you quit. It's not a race, and you don't have to get to the top the quickest. It doesn't matter if it takes you ten months or ten years. If you stay the course, if you keep plugging away at it, you will succeed. Same goes for life. When you know what you want, don't give up on it. I believe that the hurdles put in front of us are an important part of the journey, and if you want something so bad you can't sleep at night, then don't give up on it. Ask the universe for it, trust that it will happen, and then keep chipping away. Little habits every day, over time, will compound and take you closer to your goal.

What advice would you give to someone who is considering starting a network marketing business?

Do your research. Pick a company that has products that are consumable and that you trust. Make sure they have a compensation plan that rewards you based on sales volume and not recruiting.

Once you've found a company and an opportunity that excites you, jump in with both feet. The start-up costs in our industry, compared to buying a franchise or starting a traditional business from scratch, are trivial, but the opportunity is infinite. What have you got to lose? Get over yourself and stop worrying about what everyone else will think. Unless they're willing to pay your bills, their opinions don't count. I've learned to only take advice from people who've been where I want to go.

Say yes and learn later. That's what's beautiful about our business. You don't have to study for years before you earn an income. You can start earning from month one and continue to earn while you're learning and improving your skills. If you commit to becoming a professional in this industry, then the sky is the limit.

And finally, it's not a get-rich-quick business. It will take time, commitment, and courage to step out of your comfort zone. So give yourself time. When I started my business, I said I would commit for one year, and that was enough for me to fall in love. But to create a life that's unrecognisable from the one you have now, you need to allow five years. The power of compounding in this business is huge, and it takes time to compound. In our company, the secret to success is to not quit. Stay the journey and be consistent, and you will be well on your way to creating a phenomenal life for yourself and your family.

CHAPTER 10

Kristy Davidson

Life goes on whether you choose to move on and take a chance in the unknown or stay behind, locked in the past, thinking of what could've been.

Stephanie Smith

CHAPTER TEN

Kristy Davidson

What is your background?

I'm one of four children who grew up in a small country town in Victoria with a big farming influence. Since then, I've remained in small country towns not too far from where I grew up. When I completed school, I travelled to university to become a teacher. Although I knew I wanted a future of helping people learn and achieve in life; I quickly realised this was not the path I was destined to pursue, so I returned home to study community services in the disability sector.

After completing a traineeship while working in a disability-supported employee environment, I moved on to a disability employment agency where I helped people with disabilities find work in the open workforce. These roles gave me the opportunity to work hands on with people with a range of disabilities. I was also responsible for the administration of running services to support them. My next career move was to work as a business manager of a P-12 college in a town close to home, just before starting a family.

How did you get into network marketing?

Whilst on maternity leave to raise my little boy, I was offered this amazing opportunity in the form of a network marketing company and have happily not returned to the open workforce since.

I've always had a strong desire to help people, and my disability employment roles allowed me to fulfil it. When we started our family, I became a fulltime, at-home parent, as I wanted to be there for my children as they grew up and achieved all of their milestones in life. Little did I know this network marketing opportunity that was about to be presented to me would give me the opportunity to stay at home with my children and fulfil my desire to help others.

I fondly recall sitting on my lounge room floor playing cars with my almost two-year-old son, when my partner came home early from work and said two simple but life-changing words: "I quit."

He'd been at his place of work for twelve years, so I knew he hadn't made this decision lightly. However, that was only to be the first big news of the day. Reality set in, when just a couple of hours later, our daughter was born. Within a day we'd become a family with two children under two and no income.

While my partner took some time out from work to spend with our family and seek other employment options, the family budget had become very tight. It was at this time my friend sent me an invitation to a workshop she was hosting for a friend of hers. I accepted, knowing deep in my heart it was just to support her and enjoy a social outing with adult conversation, as I would not be able to make a purchase.

Accepting this invitation was the beginning of something amazing for our family. After agreeing to host a workshop for her friend, I invited all of my friends and family over to discover these products I'd so quickly fallen in love with. And of course it was another excuse for a social gathering of friends and family. Even though at the time I didn't know anything about the network marketing industry or the products, I took a huge leap of faith and decided this was something I could do for our family to loosen the budget strings a fraction. After looking at the big picture, I knew I had nothing to lose.

Having such a strong *why* and desire to change the future for our family gave me the passion to really make this opportunity work. What's so fantastic about this industry is that there's no prerequisite to be qualified in any area. It requires you to have the ability to listen, learn, and implement.

Would you talk a little about how you built up your business?

At the beginning of my journey, my sponsor had decided this business wasn't for her, so all of a sudden I was left to sort this out for myself.

There and then I had a major decision to make. I could take the easy path and quit. Say, "Oh well, I tried, and it didn't work, so I'll go back to the rat race and earn a weekly wage" or stick with it, work it out, and build myself a successful business. My partner's belief in me, and the support of my family and friends, gave me the strength to take the latter of those options and start my network marketing business.

The first step was to get out into the open world and share these products with my friends and family. I stumbled my way through my initial workshops, and in just a couple of short months achieved the first of four levels of managership within the company. I remember getting to a workshop where there were fifteen guests present and thought to myself, *Wow, this is going to be great.* I sold just one product. Chin up, I headed out to my next workshop the following day to arrive to only three guests. I went home from this workshop pleasantly surprised to have sold over $2000 worth of product. This taught me never to quit. If I hadn't shown up to that second workshop, I would not have sold anything that day, and I would have never learnt it's every bit okay not to be perfect all of the time. I also learnt that getting out there to practise my skills was important to my learning and development in this business.

I didn't know everything about the products at the time. To be honest, previous to being introduced to them, I didn't use skincare and rarely wore makeup, but the workshops did become easier. I'd made the decision to become a product of the product, by using them in our home. Then while at workshops I was able to speak from experience and the reality of the positive difference these products have made in our home.

Workshops became a vital part of my business and one I thoroughly enjoyed. It's such a passion of mine to not only introduce people to these products, but to get out there, meet new people, and change lives in so many different ways.

Leaving two gorgeous children at home gave me what some people describe as *mummy guilt.* However, due to the flexibility this business offers, I'm only out of the home at times when my children can be cared for by family and friends in their own environment. It reassured me I was doing the right thing for the right result in the end. My children love when mummy is at home, but they've also come to enjoy the times when I'm out, as this is a change to their routine and provides them with different learning experiences and social interactions.

For those times when I was working from home packing orders, calling clients, and having team meetings, I would involve them as much as possible, so they feel they're contributing to our business. I also took the opportunity around their nap times, and as they grew up, Kinder times, to work on my business. Keeping friends, family, and children involved in the business helps to prevent a resistance from them that it's taking up too much of my time and continued to improve that work-life balance.

Workshops gave me a work-life balance. As a majority of these workshops would be held in the evening, I was able to spend the whole day with my children. When they headed off to bed, I could happily head out the door to what some people may refer to as work, knowing my children were content in their own environment.

There are two main ways to be successful in this business, and workshops allowed me to fulfil the first aspect, which is building a consumer network of clients who become regular users of the products, so I devoted a lot of my time to getting this right. To this day I still hold this method in high regard. The second aspect is building the business side of things, and though I hadn't begun to do it at this point in my journey, my situation would change significantly in the months to follow.

In the next couple of months, my upline reached down to offer me some guidance and support to expand and grow my business. For this I will be forever grateful. One of the most important attributes you need in the network marketing industry is to be coachable. I was like a sponge, absorbing all of the information given to me, so I could apply this knowledge not only to my personal business. But most importantly, I'm able to pass it on to my team.

This is where I was introduced to the skill of approaching people about the business opportunity and being able to give this gift to others in order to change their lives in the way mine had already been changed forever. It not only allowed me to make new lifelong friends, it put me back in touch with friends I'd lost contact with for many, many years. Creating new friends for life is just another upside to the network marketing industry.

Who has inspired and influenced you, and why?

My children inspire me to be the best version of myself in order to show them what's possible and to never limit their dreams. I want to achieve, so they can see what it means to reach your goals no matter what. I want to provide them with the belief and knowledge that anything is possible when you put your mind to it.

My success line and team always inspire me to be the best version of myself for them. They show so much resilience and determination to achieve their goals not only for themselves, but for their teams. It inspires me to continue learning and growing. I lead by example and pave the way, just as my uplines have done before me.

What are the three main attributes you feel have helped you the most to be successful in the industry?

Success in the network marketing industry can be measured in so many different ways.

Being genuine is an attribute I value highly. Staying true to who you are and why you started and remain in this business is vital to your longevity. You need to remain focused on who you are and what you aim to achieve, so you can't be distracted or blindsided by comparing yourself to others and become someone you're not. A majority of us do this at some stage in our life or business, but it's about having the mental strength to not engage in this negative thought process, so you can move onward and upward in your journey.

Being generous can go a long way in becoming successful. Always take pleasure in the gift of giving. The more you give out to your teams, the more you receive in ways you can't even imagine. Be generous with your time for your team, take care of them, be there when they need you, but also be strong in guiding them. Respect everyone for where they are and where they want their business to go, as everyone is in this for different reasons and each journey will take a different path.

Be humble. Always focus on others and their needs, in order to help them reach their goals. No matter where they are in life or business, never say you're too busy to be there for others. Never make the business about you. It's about helping other people succeed, and in turn, seeing great rewards for yourself.

If you were able to go back and start again, what would you do differently?

My journey so far has been a rollercoaster ride, with ups and downs. However, the result at the end is well worth the ride. If I had the chance to go back, I would have summoned the courage to ask for help sooner. When I first started, I thought I should know how to succeed and believed that asking questions might make me sound silly. As much as I love this business, because it allows you to earn as you learn, and you don't need to know everything to be successful, I would have asked for assistance right at the beginning to get my journey off to a better start.

I've been an independent woman from a young age, so I believed I should be able to do everything for myself. Opening myself up to the vulnerability of asking for assistance was a big step for me but an important one, as it taught me asking for help did not make me weak. Better still, it empowered me to be a better leader.

You're not the first person to embark on the journey that is network marketing. There are people who have done it before you. They've paved the way, and to be successful you simply have to be prepared to listen and learn and follow their guidance.

So, if I were able to start again, I would put up my hand for additional guidance at the beginning, but my only real regret is that I didn't start this business five years earlier.

What would you suggest to someone just starting a network marketing business?

Having been in this business for several years now, I look back at myself in the beginning, and I feel it's evident I've learnt a great deal over this time and grown as a person. This means having to come up with just one piece of advice was a difficult task.

One of the top points is to pay your business the respect it deserves. If you treat it small, that's what you'll get out of it. But if you treat it as having the huge potential it does, this will go a long way in helping you achieve success.

Never doubt yourself. Trust that you have the skills, knowledge, and ability to be successful. If you don't have it at the beginning, trust you have the ability to learn.

Have a strong *why*. Remember why you started this business but also know that along the way, your goals will change. That's why you need to stay true to yourself.

Dream big. Without a vision of where you're going, your path will be unclear. Set your goals and work hard for them. Don't be too hard on yourself if you don't achieve your set goals. Revaluate and move on.

Look for guidance and support. You're not alone, and there's always someone there to help.

Take responsibility. Your success in this business is dependent on you and not your team.

Plug into trainings and use resources that have been created and available to you. Don't spend time recreating the wheel.

Don't judge yourself against anyone else's journey. We're all individuals wanting and heading for different goals in life.

You come from a town with a population of seven hundred. When people say they don't know anyone, or the town they live in is too small, what advice would you give?

Population is not a limitation, it's a motivation. In fact, in my case it was the driving force I needed, as I wanted to prove it's possible to set up a successful business with limited resources.

As I mentioned, I live in a small, remote country town. We have just a few shops, including a butcher, bank, chemist/post office and supermarket, a small primary school and kindergarten, and a medical centre.

I didn't see my town or surroundings as a limitation. Having such a close-knit community allowed me set up a fabulous network of clients, as I'm able to provide a personal service and products without them leaving their home or town. Providing this service on a monthly basis for reorders of products creates a residual income. Your client base is a fundamental part of your business, so treasure them and use your creativity to ensure it flourishes.

In any case, I don't believe you're going to build a sustainable business just within the town in which you reside. This business is all about building relationships and networks. Your local environment is a great basis to build a great consumer network, so use these contacts to create a network of business builders.

Structuring a large network doesn't mean you need to know everyone. It's about knowing one person who knows one person, and so on. This is a journey to build networks far and wide, not a race to the top of the company. This is where building relationships becomes a vital factor.

Living a long distance from your team and contacts means that technology becomes your best friend. Being able to work with people all over the world via phone and internet allows you to grow your business anywhere and everywhere. Take advantage of all online resources, including trainings and group sessions.

Travel is inevitable when you live in the country; however this can be a massive positive for your business. It provides a lot of time for thinking and planning. It's time to clear your head, and in my case, without children in the background. It allows you time to make coaching calls to your team and listen to personal development and positive-thinking books. Use this time to grow.

What do you attribute as the main reason you've succeeded in this industry, while others haven't?

Success means something different for every person in network marketing. Setting and reaching your own personal goals is the measure of success for me. For some it's the level they achieve in the company or how fast they're able to achieve that level. For others it might be the income level, while for some it's about how many people they've helped along the way.

For me, the main reason I've been successful in this business is because I've stayed the course I set for my journey and never quit. I've also had a goal to aspire to, and once I've reached that, I set a new one. I'm not content to stay where I am.

I really aspire to helping others, and I count it as a success for me personally, if I'm able to help someone else fulfil their hopes and goals.

I've been consistent in my activity and approach to my team. My determination has played a key role in my business and family success.

I've stayed true to myself and my journey. I've followed the blueprint of my leaders and have not been distracted by others who may think they have a shortcut or better way to the top.

As I mentioned previously, there are two main aspects to this business: building a network of consumers and a network of business builders. The ability to establish and develop both of these areas is the key to having a healthy and sustainable business.

You've changed so many people's lives with the gift of a network marketing business, so what do you think you've done that has allowed you to duplicate yourself and create such amazing leaders?

Creating a network is fun and rewarding for so many reasons, but one of the main points for me is that it has allowed me to create so many new relationships. Whether it's with strangers, family, close friends, or friends I'd fallen out of contact with.

Building and fostering a relationship with my team has allowed me to create such amazing leaders. My success came quickly, and this taught me two key lessons.

1. As my team grew at a rapid rate, I knew I couldn't do everything for everyone, so I had to apply a system that was duplicable and easy for the team to do the same. It gave me a great opportunity to step back and let my leaders lead their teams to success and believe in themselves that they could do it.

2. To reassure everyone that their journey is their own, and just because they don't reach a level as quickly as someone else, doesn't mean they're not successful or valued in this business. I reassure them that they're on the right track and assist them to set their approach to achieving their new goal.

   I've always been myself, which means being open and honest. Communication is a fundamental factor. Lines of communication should be kept open at all times.

   I believe in positivity. People feed off your vibe, so always remain positive and supportive. Each person has a different goal and journey within the same business, and you need to be mindful and respectful by allowing people to feel comfortable within their own journey.

   It's important to help others see the potential within themselves and not work their business for them. I need to show them the way and then have the courage to step back and let them forge their own path with my full backing and support.

   I do that by being reassuring and supportive. For example, if they didn't reach a goal by their set time, I let them know they haven't failed. They're still going forward, but it's time to revaluate and set a new plan/goal.

What has been the biggest benefit to your, and your family's life, because of your network marketing business?

Becoming involved in a network marketing company has changed not only my life, but the life of my family. The biggest benefits that come to mind are time and financial freedom.

I have the ability to work when and wherever I choose and generate income that will support my family.

I love how if the kids or I get sick, I don't have to call in for the day off. I choose when I work, so I can be there for my kids in their time of need. Living in a small town, I would have found it difficult to find employment and childcare that provides this kind of income. I would need to travel at least thirty-five minutes each way to a regional town centre for employment.

It has given me back the time to spend with my family. I don't have to think about getting a job from nine to five, finding daycare for my children, only seeing them before I drop them off, and then quickly while they have tea and go to bed. I've been able to be home with my children right from day one and haven't missed any of their milestones.

We as a family now have financial freedom, lifestyle choices, and a new group of amazing and supportive family and friends.

We have the ability to be able to choose what we want in life. We're no longer living from pay to pay. No more dreading opening the mailbox, because there might be a bill we can't afford to pay this week or month. Quitting wasn't an option for me. I had an income to replace and wanted to do this whilst staying at home with my young children.

I look back to when we'd only been in this business for about six months, and our oven blew up. Had this occurred twelve months earlier we would not have been in a position to replace it, until we'd spent months saving up the money, while living off meals that didn't need to be cooked in an oven. This network marketing opportunity provided our family with the ability to instantly replace the oven without saving or borrowing the money to do so. As is so often the case, the washing machine, fridge, and air conditioner soon needed to be replaced as well. I can't state strongly enough the amount of stress and anxiety that has been saved for our family by having access to income from a career I love.

We can now sit down and plan a family holiday that we want to go on, not just one we can afford after saving for years and years. We're able to provide holidays and opportunities to our children that previously would have only been hopes and dreams.

A savings account is now growing instead of spending all of our money each fortnight.

What are your top five tips for success in network marketing?

1. BE REAL AND HONEST.

    This business relies on building and nurturing relationships. You become your business. People buy from you because of your relationship and the service you provide, not solely because of the product. Being yourself is the easiest way to maintain the same standard in your business.

2. BE PREPARED TO WORK ON YOURSELF WITH PERSONAL DEVELOPMENT.

    It's the fundamental key in this business. To aspire to be your best so you can lead your team and inspire others to do the same. Be prepared to better yourself, so you can acquire even more knowledge to pass on to your teams and empower them to be better.

3. STAY THE COURSE, AND NEVER GIVE UP.

    The journey can be tough at times, but the only way to fail in this business is if you quit. That's the end of the journey and there's no road to follow. By riding out the tougher times you open the path to endless possibilities. When times get tough, go back to the basics. Revisit your *why* and find your motivation again

4. BE COMMITTED.

    When you make a decision to say yes to a network marketing business, be committed to that decision, and be committed to yourself. You may not have forty hours a week to run your business, but if you say yes and decide you have ten hours a week, then commit yourself to those ten hours and make them the most effective and productive ten hours you can provide to your business. It's not about doing everything, it's about making the decision to do something and following it through.

5. PRETEND AS IF EACH DAY OR MONTH IS YOUR FIRST.

Always remember the enthusiasm and determination with which you started your business. Call upon this if times get a bit tough. Build your business each month as if you've just started. This will ensure you have a rock-solid and sustainable business for life, no matter what people in your team decide to do. If it's meant to be, it's up to me!

In summary, I would like to say that, if you've made the decision to say YES to network marketing be committed to this decision. Keep it simple and have fun. Enjoy the journey and relish the new friendships. It's a social business, so embrace it with open arms, relax and cherish the good times. Don't make it harder than it has to be. I always say, there's nothing life-threatening in network marketing. There are no limitations. There are only excuses. Don't let the excuses become obstacles. Be clear about where you want to go, set your path to get there, and DO IT.

"You can have everything in your life you want if you will just help enough other people get what they want."

Zig Ziglar

CHAPTER 11

Lisa Ciurleo

CHAPTER ELEVEN

Lisa Ciurleo

What is your background? What was your childhood like?

I'm the eldest of the four Sanderson children and a big sister to Kimberlee, Aaron, and Paul. I grew up on a farm in Coonooer Bridge, just north of St. Arnaud in Victoria. I enjoyed all that a farm life provides. I got to drive tractors, combine harvesters, and utility vehicles. I fondly recall caring and tending to the animals, such as our working dogs, chickens, pigs, and sheep.

Though I didn't know it at the time, I realize now that growing up on the farm taught me routine, discipline, and nurturing. I had to be on time for the school bus, as I travelled 30kms each way to and from school. When the bus dropped me home, I had to feed and water the dogs and collect the eggs while feeding the chooks. During the week, the farm went like clockwork and influenced me greatly during my schooling years.

For my high school, I attended the St Arnaud Secondary College, where I decided I would go on and study at university. I loved school, and my VCE results enabled me to accept a position at Ballarat University. But after the first semester, I knew my personality wasn't suited to classroom studies. I didn't have a problem with the work. I just felt I was missing the personal interaction, and I decided I didn't want to pursue business management/ accounting as a career, as it didn't have that personal interaction as its main component.

What were some of your earlier jobs?

I was fortunate enough to get an apprenticeship back home with a local St Arnaud salon owner, Sonya Egan. I'd always dabbled in hair and makeup. I had chosen to do hairdressing as work experience while in Year 10 at school and really enjoyed it. I loved the exciting prospect of moving back home to the farm to begin learning a trade, not to mention that my boyfriend and future husband, Shane, also lived and worked in St Arnaud. It felt like it was meant to be.

From the first day on the job, I knew hairdressing was the right choice for me. I learnt so much in a short space of time. The steepest learning curve was managing social interactions. The topics of conversation in a hair salon, oh my goodness! You name, we covered it. I found out quickly that hairdressers become listeners, counsellors, and coaches, and I enjoyed helping people feel good by being a trusted listener and making them look fabulous at the same time.

I spent five years with Sonya at the salon, where I completed my apprenticeship and made lifelong friends with so many wonderful colleagues and clients. Shane and I were married in November of 2001 and were planning our future, so this was the time I started working in his family business. The family owned a supermarket, butcher shop, and hardware store in the town. The local bank had shut down and moved into the supermarket, and I was going to run that alongside Shane and his parents.

Working in a family business diversified my knowledge of business. I continued to work with Shane up until falling pregnant and giving birth to our first child, Bailey Sam Ciurleo, in July of 2003. It was just a typical country Victorian life of family, friends, and of course, sport.

In December of 2004, Shane and I made a decision to try something new and moved to Ocean Grove, on the Bellarine Peninsular. Friends of ours were building a new supermarket on the beachfront at Point Lonsdale, and we thought it was a great time for a change. I moved down there with Shane and Bailey, who was eighteen months at the time, and attempted to settle into life by the ocean. I looked forward to the challenge of treading our path together.

Early in February, 2005, my dad delivered the last trailer load of our belongings. It was about a three-hour drive from Ocean Grove to St Arnaud, and my dad had done a few back and forward trips to help us move. He was so proud of us, that we had the courage to move and was a great supporter of our decision, even though I knew he'd miss us dearly. Two weeks later, my dad was tragically killed in a car accident.

After Dad's passing, we moved back to St Arnaud to be closer to my mum in order to lend a hand. Shane helped my mum and brother, Aaron, on the farm for a few months, before getting a job in sales and marketing at a local manufacturer, while I decided to start my own salon at home, so I could work around Bailey.

I enjoyed being back in hairdressing, and eventually we settled in like we never left. Our daughter, Isabella Grace, was born in 2006, and our lives were just going along quietly, without too much fuss. In 2011 we welcomed our third child, Cooper Mark Sandy, into the world, and our little family unit was complete. Life was good, and we looked forward to the future.

How were you introduced to network marketing?

It was about October 2011 when a friend and client invited me to a party plan night for a new range of cosmetics. Now, I love finding out about new cosmetics, so I went along for a look. I took a liking to the products but took no notice of the business opportunity.

When I came home, I told Shane how much I loved the products, so he asked me for some literature on the business opportunity. After he read the literature, he asked me, "How much do you like these products, and what do your friends think of them?" When I told him again how much my friends and I loved them, and I wanted to buy more, he suggested I arrange a meeting to discuss becoming a consultant and joining the business.

Shane has a good commercial acumen, so I was guided by his suggestion. I arranged the meeting for both of us, but I had no intention of joining the business that day. Then after a couple of skinny lattes and conversation about how the business works and the steps required, Shane said to them, "Where do we sign?" I reluctantly agreed but told the girls we would catch up the following week with the documents signed. After some "robust" discussion with Shane on the way home, I was persuaded to introduce these products into the salon and to my clients. It would complement my business and potentially deliver more income. I had no idea at the time, but saying yes to this business was about to change our lives for the better.

What are your three favourite things about network marketing?

Network marketing is a fun way to connect with people. I've always enjoyed listening to the stories they have to tell. Those who know me are aware I love to join in the conversation. You know that feeling you get, when you talk to a new friend, and you feel like you've known them forever? I'm not sure if there's a word to describe that feeling, but it makes you feel glad you've made the effort to say, "Hello, I'm Lisa. Lovely to meet you."

I can't imagine how boring my life would be without meeting people, interacting with them, and discovering we share a similar passion. I'm not just talking about clients, but my business partners and their business partners. People inspire me every day, and the more people I meet, the more inspiration I draw from their stories and experiences.

I enjoy meeting new people and the social element of introducing them to my products. It doesn't feel like work in the sense that we're meeting over coffee dates, pamper nights, and wine and cheese nights. It's not a chore for me, nor is it seen as a chore for those who come along to these events. I can't think of many other business opportunities where you can grow your own business over coffee, wine, and luxury facial pampers. Any of these casual meetings can change someone's life forever. I didn't plan to join a network marketing company. I wasn't looking for an opportunity. But I'm thankful someone made an effort to invite me to a party. I'll be forever grateful for the positive effect it's had on my family's life and attempt to pay that forward in my business.

What's the biggest difference between the hairdressing industry and network marketing?

The most notable difference I've discovered is that I still make money when my hands aren't working. Hairdressers, or in fact most trades people, only get paid when they're physically working. While I loved hairdressing, I would feel the physical effects of standing on my feet all day, leaning over and cutting hair. It can be tiring. I often visited the chiropractor or physiotherapist for relief of neck, back, and shoulder pain. There was always the usual time of year when someone would come in the salon and pass on a cough or cold, so I couldn't book appointments for fear of making others sick. That meant I wasn't getting paid.

With network marketing, I can use electronic and social media to stay in touch with my customer base and keep the sales ticking over. I can be in bed with the flu, or on a beach in Fiji, and still earn an income. Consumer products are purchased on so many different platforms. E-Commerce is a continual growing market segment. I can easily adapt my network marketing business to current market trends, without having the burden of a bricks-and-mortar shop front investment to slow me down.

A majority of people say they're time poor, and time is a great commodity. Network marketing doesn't dictate opening or closing hours. I can have my products available to people 24/7 and can meet with them to discuss the business opportunity at a time that suits them. Whoever said, "Never mix business with pleasure" didn't know what they were talking about.

Who has inspired and influenced you, and why?

Like most people, I feel my parents have been the biggest influence in my life. My mum, Jenny Sanderson, taught me that modesty, conservatism, appreciation, and respect for others will carry me a long way. My dad, Mark Sanderson, was more of a risk taker and an entrepreneur, the perfect Ying to my mother's Yang. Being farmers, my parents effectively took great risks every year, as farming can be great when seasons are good and demoralizing when they're bad. I certainly inherited the entrepreneurship gene from my Dad. He was an innovative farmer who was able to identify an opportunity to improve efficiency in several areas of the farming operation.

One example that best illustrates his entrepreneurial traits was when he was sick of wearing out the points they were using to plow the paddocks before sowing and designed his own that had Tungsten applied to the tips of the points. Tungsten is a strong, abrasive, and hard metal, and it extended the lifecycle of the points they used. After proving to himself this Tungsten-tipped point was a winner, he started telling his friends and fellow farmers all about them. He was a true network marketer if there was ever one. Soon after, Dad had me working after school soldering tungsten tips to the now-patented Sanderson Point.

After selling literally thousands of these points through word of mouth and demonstrations, he had to find a manufacturer in South America to keep up with the demand. He went on to sell the rights to the design and kept a small royalty coming in. Not only did he have the skills to identify the product, he had the gift of communicating with people in such a way that they trusted what he said. Not because he was a shifty salesman but because he was genuine and passionate. That was one of the things I loved the most about him and what I can now identify as being the biggest influence in my network marketing life so far.

My husband, Shane, has also been the biggest influence in my business. I have to give credit to him for opening my eyes to the network marketing opportunity. I never saw myself as a businesswoman, even when I owned my own salon. In the early days of my network marketing business, Shane always encouraged me to treat the business seriously. He was exposed to business management at an early age, due to growing up in his family's business, and had the opportunity to learn from others as well. It taught him some valuable lessons. Shane would always listen, read, and learn about other people's businesses. It's something he encourages me to do. Shane has never said no straight away to a business opportunity. He always looks at each one objectively before ruling them out. It's that attitude that enabled us to look at network marketing, and I encourage others to do the same.

Our three beautiful children, Bailey, Isabella and Cooper inspire me every day with their enthusiasm for my business. Making their lives more positive and exposing them to some of the most amazing people and best opportunities is a dream come true.

I also have the most amazing business partners, sisterlines, and greater team members. They not only inspire me, they are a continual support and encouragement to everything I do. I love that they had the confidence to partner with me in this amazing journey to make the positive changes in our lives that network marketing provides.

How did you incorporate your network marketing business into your home salon business?

My salon was the obvious place to start introducing the products. I trusted the products and wanted to share them with my clients. It was a comfortable, low-pressure situation that helped build my confidence in the beginning of my network marketing journey. It wasn't something I pushed hard with. Sharing the products was a great icebreaker. I used samples and a *try before you buy* approach. Like almost all consumer products, there are competitive products in the marketplace, and I didn't take it personally if someone wasn't interested in buying. I knew that the more people I introduced the product to, the more interest I would get. I always had literature on hand. My salon was a great place to have the information available, as there was always time to spare while colours set. It's important to have literature available to give away to someone who shows interest in the products or the business.

If you were able to go back and start again what would you do differently?

If I was able to start again, I would have planned a transition out of my hairdressing business and into network marketing. I've been in network marketing since the end of 2011 and treated the opportunity as a part-time business for the first two years. I was new to the business and already had my own bricks-and-mortar salon. Owning my salon allowed me to feel comfortable. So while I was interested in network marketing, I admit I didn't have a hundred percent commitment to it. Even though my husband was encouraging me to treat my network marketing business seriously from the outset, my priority was hairdressing.

I trusted the products and the business opportunity, but in hindsight, I believe I lacked the self-confidence to challenge myself and what I knew to be a safe, stable business. My advice is to go on a journey of self development. To train yourself to explore and challenge your normal. I honestly believe that I stagnated in my network marketing business out of fear of the unknown. Life begins at the end of your comfort zone, and it took me two years too long to understand that.

What's great about network marketing is that the power is in your hands. I often say, "If it's meant to be, it's up to me." There are so many successful people to learn from. Networking isn't just about selling. It's about learning and sharing your, and others', experiences. I encourage you to challenge yourself every day, from day one of getting involved with your network marketing business. Treat yourself and your business seriously, and others will see you're serious about your business.

What have been some of the rewards and recognitions you've achieved in your network marketing business?

My business exploded when I committed fulltime to it in mid-2013. My family has enjoyed some amazing holidays, rewarded to me from the company. Our first trip was to Fiji. It was an amazing experience to expose my husband and children to the lifestyle network marketing can afford you. Sharing the experience with other families in network marketing was a priceless experience. We now have an annual trip away together with our network marketing business partners, courtesy of the company.

I was also fortunate enough to be awarded a trip to a Global Conference in Las Vegas, where I was a finalist at the Grand Parade of Champions for Growth and Development. This is open to all consultants in our network marketing business around the world. The Grand Parade was something out of a traditional American beauty pageant. The top twenty consultants from around the world were presented on stage in front of 20,000 people at the Garden Arena at the MGM Hotel and Casino. There I was, a mother of three who grew up on a farm in Central Victoria, on the big stage in Las Vegas.

I was awarded number eight in the world in 2014 for Growth and Development, and the company bestowed me a magnificent $5,000 tiffany ring. I've also been recognized as a leader and been awarded a five-star luxury trip to New Zealand. Network marketing companies are good at rewarding and encouraging people.

In July of 2014, on my husband's birthday, I was gifted a white Mercedes Benz by the company. I was so proud to achieve it, and it's a visual reminder of what you can achieve in network marketing and by helping others. The companies reward you for what you do. It's an amazing and uplifting experience. Sharing it with your family and your team is a special feeling.

After moving from one state to another, how did you build your business when you knew no one? What advice do you have for people who feel they don't know anyone, so they wouldn't be able to run a network marketing business?

In early 2013 we moved to Toowoomba, Queensland. It was an opportunity for Shane to further his career after recently completing a university degree to complement his experience. We approached it as a working holiday for us and decided we would have a go and get outside of our comfort zone.

This move shifted my mindset. I left behind a bricks-and-mortar salon business and moved to a town where I knew no one. All I had was my husband and three children, plus a small network marketing business that held no geographical boundaries. I knew I could use my business to meet people and expose my products and business to a different network. I also knew I was going to hear rejections, and it would hurt.

It took me three to six months to finally decide to crawl out of my shell and start telling people in my new hometown about my business. I followed the same basic pattern. I organized coffee dates, workshops, cheese and wine nights, fundraising events for the school, and basically any excuse to get people together and meet them. I found a confidence and strength I didn't realize I had, because I was genuine and passionate, just like my dad. I had this amazing realization that all of this time I was learning and preparing for the moment when I became a true entrepreneur, just like my dad.

I was doing what I loved, meeting new people, socializing, and just enjoying the opportunities and experiences presented to me and my family by moving outside of my comfort zone. There are opportunities everywhere. If you tell yourself you can't, you won't. Accept rejection. Use it as energy to ask the next person, and keep asking until someone says yes. You can run a network marketing business from anywhere, any time. I'm living proof. If you believe in your heart you can, you will.

What great daily tips do you have for someone who's just starting their network marketing business?

The one thing I do, and encourage others to do every day, is to invest in yourself. Knowledge is power. Every day I read an article, a quote, or a chapter of a book I can draw inspiration and knowledge from.

I recommend you look at your social media interactions and take stock of the people and companies you follow. Facebook is a great example of a news source that can affect your mindset. Use Facebook to follow inspirational people, fearless leaders, and entrepreneurs. Decrease your exposure to negativity. Identify the negative influences in your life and take steps to change or remove them. Every day I invest in positive people and stories from all forms of media.

I also reach out every day and contact someone for advice, an opinion, or to encourage my business partners. I'm a big believer in paying it forward. Whatever support I give my business partners, I get back double. It's an important element to any network marketing business. You certainly achieve more working together with others. The gains are not just financial. The experience of making someone feel good about the decisions they've made, or have to make, is uplifting for both of you.

I'm fortunate to have three amazingly supportive people as my business mentors, who I can reach out to for help and advice. Rachel Lubcke is a hard-working mother of four kids. We don't just talk business. Were like family and help each other through a variety of situations. Rachel runs her own successful network marketing business around her children. She's an amazing, patient, kind, and caring person I learn a lot from.

Another of my business partners is Angela Weston. Ange left behind a high-flying global role with a fashion label to concentrate on her network marketing business. If that wasn't inspiring enough, she's also a mum of two kids and is such a helpful person I'm grateful to have not only have in my business, but my life.

I'm fortunate enough to call Debbie Loughnane a business partner and a friend. Deb is a calming, measured influence who often guides me when I'm unclear because of the emotions I feel around issues in my business.

All of these women love and support me, and I encourage anyone entering into network marketing, to find a support network that works for them, and to never be afraid to ask.

I make sure I offer that same support to my amazing team. There's not enough room in a book for me to express my gratitude, love, and admiration for the people who are not only my business partners, but sisterlines who truly inspire me every day with their determination.

Invest in yourself and pay it forward.

What does your future look like now because of network marketing?

Network marketing has changed our lives forever for the better. Financially, we now have options, and can provide opportunities for our children. Instead of scraping through with bills and mortgage repayments, we can invest in our children's future. And when I use the term invest, I'm not referring to trust funds. I mean education and life experiences, relationships, and friendships.

I can spend more time with them as they grow up and guide them through childhood. I can go on family holidays and allow them to meet the children of my business partners, so they can develop friendships and relationships with people outside of their immediate school circle. I can invest in top-quality education and healthcare for my family and give them every opportunity to do what they love in their working lives, just as I do. Our future is about enjoying the opportunities network marketing can give and about sharing those opportunities with others.

There's also the opportunity to invest in yourself with a little self indulgence. Who doesn't love a little retail therapy to reward yourself for a good day's work? My business allows me to do that and not dread the credit card statement at the end of the month. My husband and I are able to plan and invest for our financial future, as well as the future success of my business. I plan to continue to be a successful network marketing business owner well into the future, and I want to continue to inspire those who are interested in doing the same. I love what I do.

I'm so grateful to be surrounded by the most amazingly supportive family, friends, and business partners. They are my future-makers, and together we've provided each other the opportunities to decide our futures. I can only thank those fearless women who said yes to network marketing before me and blazed the trail that offered me this wonderful opportunity. Now I want to provide the same opportunity to as many people who have the courage to say YES.

*"Don't put the key
to your happiness in
someone else's hand."*

Unknown

CHAPTER 12

Michelle Ryan

CHAPTER TWELVE

Michelle Ryan

Tell me about your early life.

Ever felt like you didn't fit in? That was me. My childhood consisted of lots of ups and downs. My mother left my abusive father when I was just a baby and relocated from the sunny state of Queensland to the southern suburbs of Melbourne. My mum's new boyfriend was a drunk, and a violent one at that. Probably not unlike my own father. Some memories never leave you, and seeing my mum's blood on the doorstep is something I will never forget. It's the sort of thing no child should see, let alone understand. It was the elephant in the room, never discussed. Not with anyone.

We lived in the "Pines" in Frankston, a well-known housing commission area. My mother is a feisty woman, and even though she would bear the brunt of her boyfriend's drunken rages, she also had a defiance about her, something that wouldn't be broken. This was not a good time for our little family, and the damage still affects some of us all of these years later. I came away what I consider relatively unscathed from our years with him. I had his mother, I called Nanna, who loved and adored me. My Nanna is still a voice in my head today. She had great wisdom and taught me so much. She passed away Christmas of 1997. I still miss her.

Everything changed in a big way when my mother met the man who was to become her next husband and my stepfather. Syd was a recently divorced, feisty, yet fun-loving Scot. I didn't really know any other man as my father. My biological father lived in Sydney and died when I was just seven.

This man became the stability we all needed. He adored my mother. He'd stir her up with silly jokes, which ended with her screeching and us laughing. He was a tough parental male figure who didn't take any rubbish but was always funny and generous. My primary school years were made up of being *that* kid at school. The one who's not popular but not unpopular. An average girl in every way. My parents worked long hours, and we were required to cook and clean regularly, always doing jobs and chores for the household.

I would be the coffee maker when my parents' friends would come over. We still laugh at the stories of my mum screeching in her high-pitched voice, "Michelle! Michelle! Make us a cuppa, will ya?"

I spent most of my school years just getting by, with my school reports mostly below average. On reflection, I find it strange, as I love to learn. As an adult I've been an avid reader, particularly history and anything based on real people and real-life issues. I'm always looking to learn about everything I can, like a sponge. I read up on everything and anything.

In high school I asked my careers teacher for help in deciding whether I should pursue the police force or nursing. His reply was that I was too short for the police force, which back in the mid-eighties had height requirements, and I didn't have the brains for nursing. He added that my best bet in life was to find a bloke who would marry me. This was a defining conversation. This teacher's reply made such an impact on me that I'm now thankful. I owe my thanks to him. This simple comment has been a strong driver for me to succeed and desire more for my life.

I started Year 11 and knew months into it I was going to struggle. I hadn't put much effort in until then and just didn't have the knowledge as to what to do. Plus, I had struggled with bullying for a solid eighteen months at my new school, so I was keen for a way out. At this point the bullying and other dramas going on became intolerable. Adults I'd trusted weren't guiding me, and I'd lost faith.

My parents were having major dramas of their own and were in the process of losing every cent they had due to a failed business, so my teenage problems just didn't rate. They ended up losing the business, the house, and eventually their marriage. I was lost, lonely, and had no clue what to do. I just knew deep inside myself there *had* to be more to this thing called life. I had a deep knowing that I couldn't follow the path of what was considered the normal pattern of events, which was to leave school, get a job, marry, and have kids. I did want these things, but I wanted them on MY terms.

How did you move on from that situation, and what were some of your earlier jobs?

The little fire inside of me told me there had to be more to life. I had just turned eighteen, and I was desperate to escape. I was terrified this was it. Most of the girls I knew already had children, but I knew that wasn't for me. Not at eighteen, anyway. I wanted to see the world. I questioned whether my life was going to be stuck like that forever. Would I have to make do? Would I have to settle? I questioned everything, and although I didn't have answers I decided making a change was the quickest way to make something else happen.

So, I left. I ran off to Queensland but didn't tell my family until I'd already made it there. I worked in a few nightclubs around surfers, became involved in the "Miss" pageants of the time, and hung around all of the cool and beautiful people sun-baked on the beach or at hotel pools during the day. I cocktail waitressed at night and danced the early mornings away at clubs like Melba's, Players, and Cocktails and Dreams.

When my new housemate moved in, I was thrilled. Annette had something about her. She was a photographer for a family portrait firm and was making good money. One day she asked me if I could help her at her next shoot. "Oh, yes!" was my reply. I couldn't have been happier. This was an awesome experience, and I quickly learned the ins and outs. She taught me what I needed to know. She also helped guide in other areas, such as fashion, skincare, and makeup, and how to appreciate the finer things life could offer. She showed me there were other worlds out there and so many possibilities.

The money I made working with her was great and so much more interesting than cocktail waitressing. My boss at the club told me I should go back to Melbourne. She didn't think I was the type of girl who would be okay on the Gold Coast. Too many weird men, drugs, and dead-end lives leading to nowhere. Something about how she said this had me take notice I didn't even drink alcohol in those days, and after a waitress went mysteriously missing, I took her words of advice and returned to Melbourne.

I was able to start up with the same photography business as Annette, and I worked hard for a year or so in order to prove to myself I was more than the dumb blonde my chauvinist careers teacher insinuated I was. By the time I was twenty one, I had the last laugh on him, as I was making more money than any school teacher could.

This was a pivotal point for me. The real gift was that I realised wanting more and having more wasn't just a dream. It was real. You can have what you want. You just have to be willing to put yourself out there.

By the time I was twenty four I was married and had two small children. My husband, Steve, worked for a phone company as a linesman. He was a little moody, but to me that was normal. However, as the years rolled on he became terribly depressed and at times wouldn't shower or dress for weeks. He wanted to be isolated, so we moved to a big country town in Victoria, where he became overwhelmed with work stress. His depression became deeper and deeper. He took meds and did counselling, but it wasn't helping. He was offered a redundancy, and he took it.

Meanwhile, I got a job as a trainee mortgage broker. I loved the work, but of course I had my difficulties with home life, juggling kids, work, and Steve's illness. It was possibly the hardest time of my life. I was at my wit's end. A few days before our son's fourth birthday, my husband and I had a fight. I'd had enough of trying to help someone who didn't want it, and he'd had enough of feeling helpless. He left the house and called me from a telephone box to say goodbye. He told me there and then he couldn't do life anymore and was going "end it all."

To be honest, what he meant didn't really sink in at first. Not really. He wanted me to meet him to talk and maybe "go with him." These words hit me and made me understand in a split second this was very real and very serious. I made sure I wasn't alone or going anywhere on my own to meet him.

You never know where this type of situation may take you or how it will pan out, but I'm so grateful I'm here, because I followed my instinct and said, "No, I'm not leaving the children. I want to live. I'm sorry if you don't." I had to disconnect myself from the reality. I initially froze but then called for help. I chose my children, and I chose *me*.

Our family, friends, and police searched for him, knowing this was a life-and-death situation. It took us two days of panic, stress, driving, and searching to find his body. Sadly, he was just a few minutes away from our home. It was 1998, and I was twenty-seven years old with two children, seven and three. When I look back, I wonder how I coped. I think I lived in shock on some sort of auto pilot, like a robot, for what seemed like forever.

I carried guilt and blame for his death for many years. I felt I should have stopped him. I was told by people close to me I should have stopped him. That burden was a big one to carry. I was watched, judged, and made to be wrong about everything I did from that day forward. On reflection, I quite possibly still am, but when you make choices that are right for you it doesn't matter what others say, think, or feel. Another awesome lesson that serves me today and into my future.

A few years later I married my second husband, Rod, who was a rock for me after Steve's death. I'd met him when I started in the mortgage business before Steve died. He and Rod had been friends with common interests in gold prospecting.

In 1999, Rod had been given an opportunity to build up a mortgage broking business. He was great at the job but paperwork wasn't his thing, so that's where I came in. I liked paperwork and organising. We started dating and quickly fell in love but were hit with loads of self-righteousness and judgement because of our relationship. But we followed our hearts and did what we wanted and not what was expected. I was hated and judged. I was closed out by family and friends. I lost people I thought cared about me, because I made the choice to move forward with my life. I'm happy to say I don't currently hold onto the pain from this experience, but it took a long time to learn how to feel happy about even the simplest of joys.

Rod and I had a baby girl and married in 2000. The mortgage broking industry went through massive growth during our early days. Rod and I played our part in building the company. We recruited hundreds. Some became successful, and some did not. We tripped and fell a number of times, messed things up, got out of our depth sometimes, made emotion-based decisions that didn't turn out how we wanted, and went through periods when we didn't even know what to do. Wow, what a ride!

We worked hard, often until the early hours of the morning. Success had found us. This was more like I'd dreamt all of those years ago as a teenage girl. We built a home, had a nice life, and a beautiful family. We had another baby girl who completed our family. We were able to provide a comfortable life for ourselves. We drove nice cars and lived in nice houses, our children attended some of the most prestigious schools, and we travelled often, which included a five-week European family holiday. We had it all. We even had an annuity income, which meant even if we went on holidays, money still came in. How does it get any better than that?

However, the situation began to change. We began to change, and as a result, what we wanted from life began to change as well. Previous business and personal decisions were no longer working for us. It was a slow decline and one that until the end we didn't comprehend how little control we had. The annuity income was not what we thought it was, and as it turns out we could only have it while still working in the company. We couldn't will it to our children, and we couldn't sell our business, either. Our passion was dying, and it showed in every aspect of our business.

We were stuck there with golden handcuffs. This became a sticking point and de-motivated us. The lack of control started to become a problem. We were approaching forty, and priorities change when you have a family and get to this age. After much thought, discussion, dramas, changes, and with some fifteen years in the business, we decided to opt out. To do this, we cut ties with people we were in business with and had come to care about and just walk away with NO money, NO income, and NO shares in the business we'd invested in so heavily financially, emotionally, and personally. This was the boldest and scariest move we'd ever made.

What we did come away with was a whole lot of real-life skills that we knew if we backed ourselves, we could build again. We were the wiser for it. Sometimes the hard choices are the best ones, even when you don't think so at the time. You have to follow what you really want, bite the bullet, and do what's best you, not everyone else.

The opportunity came about for Rod to get involved in the real estate field, something we both had a natural interest in and worked hand in hand with our mortgage knowledge. He quickly found a position to get started, and I went into managing a café my family had bought. Managing the restaurant was another really tough gig. The hours were crazy, and the stress was overwhelming. Rod was doing okay, but he was new, so there was some groundwork to be done. You don't replace the sort of income we had that easily. The road back to success was going to be a long one, and at times it felt like a daunting prospect to start again in our early forties, in debt up to our eyeballs, with three children still at home.

What we did know was that neither us enjoyed the idea of working in a nine-to-five job until retirement. Clocking in and out of a daily job was not something we'd done for many years, and if it wound up that we had to, we wanted to do it on our own terms. The most valuable lesson learnt from my life and its dramas was that I prefer to have choice. We all have it, but it takes courage to use it. Choice is a gift. Grab it and run!

My hubby was approached by an older gentleman who was planning his retirement. He had some success with his independent real estate business for a few years and was looking for someone to move into a succession role. He'd done his homework and quickly found Rod was awesome at what he did. It was a readymade small business that had reasonable results and low overheads for what was a single operator in a niche market.

So Rod took the offer and became the owner of this little independent called HBA Realty. My family sold the café, and I moved back into the office manager role for our new real estate business. We took it from a home office-run real estate business to now having a head office in our local community and the strongest sales market. The business has five agents, two office support staff, and a rental manager. We're working to establish in other areas with plans for more offices. I'm so pleased to say that HBA Realty is, and will continue to achieve, amazing results, because we know we have what it takes to be the best we can be, but mostly because we make a daily, conscious choice to live life the best we can.

How did you go from real estate to network marketing?

After two years in our new real estate business, we wanted to build the annuity income that had eluded us before. The real estate agency had been building up a rental book, however we wanted another option. Another line of income that would help create what we'd always wanted. An annuity income we could will, and a legacy for our children. I wanted something I could contribute more to. Something I could do that helped others, was fun, and would provide an income that could grow. It would be an addition to what we were doing with the real estate business and something I could do regardless of my age. Something with longevity.

I'd kept in touch with a woman I'd helped with home loans over the years. From the moment we met years ago, I was inspired by her determination. She was feisty but also fun. That woman is Debbie Loughnane. She'd been on board for six months with a network marketing business that involved skin care and makeup and was doing well with it. She was the first Australian Independent Consultant for this global brand. Over the seven years I've known her, I watched her business grow and grow and grow.

Actually, Debbie asked me to join her business when we initially met seven years previous, and one other time, but I only said yes a year ago. Why didn't I accept the opportunity the other two times it was offered? Why did I wait so long?

First, I had loads of self-doubt, and to be honest, when she first made the offer I thought this annuity income thing was under control with the business we had. It wasn't until it all fell apart that I looked at other options. I couldn't see the possibilities.

The second time Debbie rang, the timing wasn't right. I was still reeling from the financial turmoil, and frankly we had a tough year or two of coming to terms with the situation. It was taking its toll. I'd been a mess. Somehow all of the "wrongness" of me, as well as the "wrongness" of my husband and our choices, had made me ill. I was hospitalised five times. Not only that, my stepfather became ill and died. I was broken. We both were.

I also had reservations about this network marketing stuff and how people I'd come across hid what their business was. No one wants that invite for dinner, only to have to sit through an uninvited, unsolicited "presentation." The stigma attached to network marketing has been a tough one for years, but then on second thought, real estate agents and mortgage brokers are also at the top of that list, aren't they?

Frankly, the attraction to the annuity and incentive trips at my ripe old age of forty five was too inviting, and I noticed that others in Debbie's team are good, genuine people from all walks of life. Not every salesman is a *shonk*, and not every network marketer is going to trick you to watch their presentation.

I've always enjoyed a good income and what it can do for me, but I'm mostly surprised by the growth I've had. My personal growth has been my biggest gift so far, and I'm so very grateful for Debbie and introducing me to the world of network marketing. I'm inspired and am looking forward to where this journey takes me.

How has your life changed since getting into network marketing?

The personal growth and friendships made have been amazing. My ability to help others who are, or have been, travelling my old path is a great driver. I've conquered troubled times and drama, and my self-doubt has all but disappeared. My self-esteem is improving in leaps and bounds I've learnt more about myself than I thought possible and have a renewed love of life. I became fearful of dying broke like my stepfather did, and I won't waste another minute regretting anything I do. I chose the company and Debbie, because they're proven. Most of all, I choose myself!

I didn't want to be part of a short, hot business that fizzled once the excitement wore off. So the choice was a no-brainer. The company I'm involved with has thirty five years in business. It has thousands of success stories from all over the globe and offers you as little, or as much, as you're prepared to grab and run with. It doesn't matter what shape, size, age, colour, or gender you may be, you can use this opportunity to better your life.

I was amazed by the diversity of Debbie's team when I went to my first conference she holds annually. The energy in the room was amazing, and the support they provide for each other is fantastic. They share information and strategies for success openly with one another. There were mums breastfeeding babies, toddlers playing on the floor, teenagers sitting with their mothers, and husbands and partners supporting and becoming part of the team. It was a breath of fresh air, so much so, that my eldest daughter, Jacinta, took the opportunity to join my team. As a young mum of two gorgeous boys, she works her business around her life. On her terms! My husband joined my team, because he saw the possibilities and just loves getting his cheques in the mail.

The possibilities are endless. My opportunity to help others and for more personal growth is all before me. I celebrate the small wins and look forward to the big ones.

Who has inspired you, and why?

My children, Jacinta, Shannon, Chelsea and Isabel. Regardless of what happens in life, they've rolled with the punches just like we have. I appreciate the hard work, encouragement, and blind faith of my eldest daughter, Jacinta, She's such a gorgeous mum to her boys, and her determination is inspiring. As we build our businesses together, we will have so many fun, crazy, and incredible times.

My son, Shannon. His love and respect for me is such a comfort. I've watched him grow into an impressive man. His caring, love, and respect for the women in his life has me bursting with pride. I appreciate him being the wonderful man he is.

My daughter, Chelsea, is a game-changer. A young women with a beautiful presence. The makings of a leader and someone who cares enough to help others. Watching her blossom into a strong, caring, and powerful woman is such fun for me. I appreciate her love, respect, and friendship

My youngest daughter, Isabel. She's so special, emotionally intelligent, and caring at such a young age. I've watched her grow and develop into a graceful young lady. She's such a joy. I will always cherish her smile and love.

My adoring husband, Rodney. His love and adoration for me is clear. He's never doubted me and always supported me. I'm a wild, wilful, and independent woman who takes a very strong and resilient man to be able to handle. I appreciate him standing by me, even when others didn't, don't, or wont. He's my friend, lover, and soul mate. I love him.

What are your top five tips for success in network marketing?

1. BELIEVE IN YOURSELF.

    YOU are the key to everything you wish for.

2. THROW YOURSELF INTO YOUR NEW VENTURE LIKES IT'S THE NEW LOVE IN YOUR LIFE.

    Give it the time, attention, and consideration it requires to grow, just like you would a new romance

3. LIFE NEVER TURNS OUT HOW YOU PLAN, SO BE OPEN TO ALL POSSIBILITIES.

    Good, bad, right, or wrong, it's all about how you look at it. Identify the gift in every situation, and be grateful for what you learn.

4. BE PASSIONATE.

    Passion to me doesn't mean hounding everyone you meet and badgering them. There's nothing more off-putting than someone trying to SELL you something. We all avoid those types, don't we?

    Success doesn't come from the glossy brochure. It comes from setting targets, taking action, and asking questions of yourself. So dig deep and be honest. Are you doing what makes you happy?

5. GO BACK TO TIP ONE AND REPEAT.

CHAPTER 13

Rachel Lubcke

"Sometimes the smallest step in the right direction ends up being the biggest step of your life. Tip toe if you must. But take the step."

Naeem Callaway

❧

CHAPTER THIRTEEN

Rachel Lubcke

What is your background?

I thought I had my career planned out. I'd always had a fascination and love of babies, pregnancy, and all things maternal. I'd dreamed of being a midwife from the age of ten. Immediately after high school, I begrudgingly undertook the three-year Bachelor of Nursing degree required to enable me to undertake my beloved Graduate Diploma of Midwifery.

I completed this in just twelve months and thoroughly enjoyed my craft as a midwife, especially in the first few years when shift work was not an issue for my husband and me. This soon changed, however, with the birth of our first child, Ethan, and I was faced with the financial need to return to work, just sixteen months after his birth. This is when the shift work, nightshift, and weekend work cut into family time and took its toll. I no longer enjoyed my craft as I once did. It had all become about my little family and the need to be home with them.

Six months later, we were excited to be pregnant with our second child, Grace. I would count down the days until I went on maternity leave, as what had once excited me about my job was now just a means of income. This saddened me. I never imagined feeling this way about midwifery care. I was involved in the most magical time in families' lives, and all I wanted to do was to be home with mine.

Again, I had to return to work when Grace was sixteen months old, but this time it was even more difficult being away from my babies. I was enjoying my work less and less, but I couldn't see how that was going to change. I was a midwife. This is what I had wanted since I was a child. Everyone knew me as *The Midwife*. There was nothing I could do, or so I used to tell myself. This was what I had studied so hard for, so this is what I thought I needed to do for the rest of my life.

How did you get into network marketing?

We wanted a third child, and I felt the only way out was to get pregnant again and take up some more maternity leave. It was right about then my life was forever changed, and network marketing took me by surprise. I wasn't looking for this business, but it found me, and I'm forever grateful it did. If you'd told me five years ago that I would be an Executive Regional Vice President in my own successful network marketing business, I would have laughed in your face. Never in my wildest dreams could I have imagined the wonderful position I find myself in today.

But that's what I love about network marketing. Anyone can do it. I've always said I'm not a salesperson, as I had never sold anything to anyone in my life. I looked at vaginas and breasts for a living, so the only thing I knew how to sell was having a baby and breastfeeding. But that's the great thing about network marketing. It's all about sharing. Sharing an opportunity, sharing a product, and ultimately, sharing a lifestyle.

I was introduced to this incredible business five years ago through a girlfriend, and I immediately fell in love with the products after trying them at a presentation. I listened intently to my beautiful sponsor, Angela, talk that night about all of the premium products. But I especially took note of the business opportunity that came with them, and the chance to earn an additional income stream. I remember thinking in my head, *Maybe I could do this on the side and earn a bit of extra cash*. But I still didn't fully *believe* I could do it, or that it would work. So I let it go for a while and enjoyed the products as a client for four months.

In that time, people commented on a daily basis about how well I was looking and asked me what it was I was using. I then found myself recommending our products to people on a daily basis. It was at this point my close high school friend, Natalie Brown, joined the business and encouraged me to do the same. So after four months, I figured I could join this company with products I was already so passionate about, utilise the discount for myself, and earn an extra couple of hundred dollars a month. I could see this would be a great way to supplement my income and allow me to be home longer with my babies, which is the crux of why I do this business.

The icing on the cake was when my accountant husband, Shane, read the success plan and said, "Rach, it's a no-brainer!" He pointed out how low risk the initial start-up costs were, and that there were no real overheads. The worst that could happen was that we would be left with products we loved and used anyway. So I excitedly jumped in, and people started asking to join my business as they fed off my excitement and love of the products.

The business then took on a life of its own. I couldn't believe it when after just seven months, I was not only pregnant with baby number three, but I was an area manager.

This replaced the income I was earning, which had taken me four years at university to achieve. So between working as a midwife two days a week, being a wife and mother, and all of the commitments that came with those roles, I continued to build up an incredible network and earn a wonderful income. Most importantly, however, I was also able to continue to build on our family. That became my mantra and my signature statement: "I'm building a business whilst building a family".

By the time Ava, our third child, was born, I was not only replacing my income as a midwife, but I continued to get paid that wage every month, long after my eight weeks of paid maternity leave ran out. This was a huge revelation and turning point for me in my business, as I realised what I could achieve if I really gave this business all I had and made it my plan A.

So I took the two years of maternity leave on offer and just shared this amazing network marketing vehicle with more people, all the while taking Ava with me and breastfeeding. This is something I couldn't do in my job. I could not take my baby to work strapped to me in a birth suite for an eight-hour shift, but I could in my business.

How has network marketing changed your life?

I could work any way I wanted, and that's exactly what I did. I structured my entire business around my life and family, with my children and husband being front and centre. I was, and still am, there for every school drop off and pickup, which has been absolutely priceless. I know this would not have been possible had I not said yes to this business. I can take my children to ballet, tennis, footy, playgroup, and Kinder, all whilst building a million-dollar business.

The next turning point in my business journey was when I became a Regional Vice President (RVP). Not only did this bring with it a brand-new Mercedes Benz, greater success, and further financial security, it also brought baby number four. I discovered I was pregnant, three days before becoming an RVP. I went from replacing a fulltime monthly midwife's wage, to tripling it. But more importantly, I've been able to help so many other women and men in my organisation come home to their babies and live a life of their design, where work comes second to family.

Our fourth child, Ivy, was born April of 2014, a few months before I helped my beautiful friend and business partner, Lisa Ciurleo, elevate to Regional Vice President. This is, without a doubt. my biggest business highlight to date, and that I was able to be at home with my newborn baby while coaching and supporting Lisa and her team to elevate and succeed, was priceless.

My business tripled whilst I was able to take time out to have my baby, be a mum, and concentrate on our new family of six. How does it get any better than that?

Network marketing has given my family and me financial choice and security, but most importantly, it has enabled us to grow our family and give back time with our precious babies. We've been able to move back to the town we grew up in, build our dream house, and I get to be front and centre as the stay-at-home mum I always wanted to be.

I still love the craft of midwifery, and it will always hold a special place in my heart, but the workplace environment is regimented and rigid, which is not conducive to a young family. I pinch myself every day that the business I've created for myself is what I get to do for a living. As a midwife, I was involved in an intimate time in people's lives with the birth of a child, and I got to make a difference for one day. Now I get to make a difference *every* day, both in my business and at home.

Who has inspired and influenced you, and why?

I've always admired stay-at-home mothers, and I was so privileged to have my own mother home with me whilst I was little. This was a great driving force for me being so passionate about being there for our children. My beautiful mother-in-law, Betty, was also a stay-at-home mother of four, and since both Shane and I had that growing up, it was something we wanted to pass on to our children.

In terms of business prowess, both my mother, Sandy, and father, Ian, were involved in a few different business ventures as I grew up. My good old-fashioned work ethic comes from them both and definitely added to the intrigue and excitement of creating a business for myself.

My family has been incredibly supportive of everything I've ever undertaken in my life, and the mutual respect both of my parents instilled in my brother, Mitchell, and me, not only for each other but for everyone we meet, has served us both well in being the best versions of ourselves. They say you're a product of your parents, and I completely agree. Without their love, guidance, and life lessons I apply in my business every day, I would not be where I am today.

My husband, Shane, and I have been together for twenty-four years, and he's been an incredible influence in my life. We're best friends, and everything we've done has been done together. From travelling the world, learning from third-world countries, and building a beautiful family of little humans, to standing beside me every step of the way in this business, he is my rock.

In terms of my business, there have been so many influential people along the way. First, my amazing sponsor and upline, Angela. To be able to watch this incredible woman build such a successful business right in front of my eyes and rise through the ranks of the company when I was still a little sceptical, helped me believe it may just be possible for me as well. Ange always leads by example and has been an incredible leader and support along my journey. I will be forever grateful for the gift she's given my family and me.

Of course, none of this would have been possible if it wasn't for the fierce and fabulous Debbie Loughnane saying YES to this opportunity for all of us, eight years ago. Deb is such a pioneer in the network marketing industry, and she's been such an inspiration to me from day one. What she's created for us all here in Australia is a legacy that we can now pass on to our children, and their children.

Most of my inspiration, however, comes from my diverse and humble team of business partners. I seriously have the best team of women and men in business with me, and they all inspire me every day to be the best leader I can. I could not have built such a successful organisation and elevated to Executive Regional Vice President without these key leaders and their teams: Lisa, Shane, Pru, Cheryl, Maree, Colin, Kim, Hayley, Rose, Sharon, and Kristy. I will be forever grateful to these people, along with their teams, and EVERYONE else in my incredible success line. THANKYOU! Together we are better.

I would also like to take this opportunity to thank my lifelong friend, and business sisterline, Natalie Brown, for all of her support. Nat, along with my family, have been there from day one, and she believed in me so many times when I didn't believe in myself. To be able to share this journey with someone I've known since I was twelve years old, has been incredible.

What are your three favourite things about network marketing?

1. Being able to create a residual income.

    How smart is network marketing? You do the work once, yet you get rewarded for a lifetime with a residual income. It's such a smart, savvy, and simple way of earning a living. In the beginning, I never really understood a lot about how that worked, but it didn't matter. That's what's so great about this industry. You just need to have a fantastic product you use and believe in, and the rest will follow. I will never forget waking up one morning, very early on in my business, and my first-ever online reorder had occurred overnight. I excitedly yelled out to my husband, "I just earned a hundred dollars while I was sleeping!"

2. Time leveraging and flexibility.

There are no limits to how you run your network marketing business, logistically or otherwise. That's why I love this industry so much. It's flexible, and the ability to leverage time is what makes it so attractive to people like myself. I was able to fit this business into the nooks and crannies, around work and life commitments, before being able to make it my fulltime 'job.' I can run my business from my couch with my laptop and phone. I can have international calls with business partners in my car before school pickup. I can work when I want and never miss special occasions with family and friends ever again. And it's effort-based. What you put in you will get back. I write the rules, office hours, and my pay cheque.

3. It's duplicable:

Probably the smartest aspect about networking marketing is that it's duplicable. It's an effective word-of-mouth distribution system that everyone can do, so anyone can become hugely successful. It's all about having an experience, recommending it to others, and them doing the same thing. That's it. We all start in this industry alone. But by sharing the business model with a few people, who shared it with a few people, and so on, and so on, you build an incredible network that then turns into hundreds, thousands, and eventually millions.

I love how you talk about being a midwife, and that it was amazing to be a part of someone's most special time when they're bringing a child into the world, but it's only for one day, whereas in network marketing you get to help people forever. Tell us more about that.

As a midwife, I would often meet a couple the day they became parents. I'd help them for that one special day of their lives as their babies were born. If I was lucky, I may have looked after them once or twice more on the postnatal ward, but that's where the relationship often ended.

I'm a nurturer by nature, and I love that in my business I get to help people in an ongoing capacity. Whether it's from a product point of view where I've made someone feel good about the way they look and feel for the first time, and can continue to provide that service, or being able to bring mums and dads home to their babies, the long-lasting positive effects of this business make me so incredibly proud, every day, of what I do.

One of my greatest highlights to date was when my dear friend and business partner, Lisa Ciurleo, promoted to Regional Vice President. Not only did I get to hand her the keys to her own brand-new Mercedes Benz, I was also able to help her reach a level in her business, where she never has to return to her previous job of hairdressing if she doesn't want to.

Lisa and her husband, Shane, were such a great support to me as we elevated to Region, and I'm so honoured I've been able to play a part in bringing their family some financial freedom and choice. That we get to help others on a daily basis in this business is why I'm so passionate about the industry. Being able to watch Lisa change her family's life and then to change other people's lives within her team, and our greater organisation, is nothing short of humbling.

I've had business partners ring me with excitement after reaching Area Manger level and say, "I've just dropped my days at work, and now I only work two days a week. Thank you for giving me this opportunity".

Every day, more and more people have their lives changed within my network, whether through getting great skin and feeling good, creating a residual income, or completely changing the course of their lives for the better. And it still blows my mind that all of this is occurring, because I had the courage to say yes to a network marketing business four and a half years ago.

What would you suggest to someone who's just starting a network marketing business?

Jump in with both feet, and don't hold back!

We're all nervous when we start a new venture, especially starting up your own business. But this industry is all about getting out there and talking to as many people as you can and sharing an opportunity. This industry is a numbers game. The more people you talk to, the more people may join your business, which in turn leads to a greater residual income, and the more lives you change.

Plug into all resources available to you, and be a sponge.

In this industry, we learn as we earn. Don't get hung up on all of the ins and outs in the beginning. Just be a product of your product, and keep talking about and sharing the opportunity and products. The rest will follow. Once you build momentum in this industry and keep it going, you'll have a rock-solid business.

Don't over-think it.

Trust in the product and business model that has you so excited, and share that with people.

How do you stay motivated, and how do you get others to stay motivated?

I lead by example. I try and do at least thirty minutes of personal development each day in the form of reading or listening to audio tapes that feed my mind with positivity and help me think in abundance and possibility. I encourage all of my team to do the same. When you have the right mindset, you can be an unstoppable force to be reckoned with in this business, attracting other likeminded souls into your path to allow the sharing of an opportunity.

Learning all about the industry is another great way to motivate yourself and stay excited about the industry. It reaffirms why you do what you do and validates it to others. We always say you need to be a product of the product in whatever it is your business is selling, but you also need to be a walking recommendation for network marketing.

Plugging in and showing up to *all* trainings on offer is a must. We all need motivation. It's not roses all of the time, just as in normal life. However, the difference is that the lows in a network marketing business are far less of a concern than they can be in traditional business and employment. And the great thing is, when you do get in a business slump, just go and talk to more people, share the opportunity, and it can soon be rectified. You actually have so much more power and control in this industry than in traditional business and employment.

If you were able to go back and start again, what would you do differently?

I would have jumped in straight away and not waited four months. I would also let go of the preconceived ideas I had in my head about network marketing and how people might react to me doing it, and just get out there.

I was fortunate in the first year of my business that each person who joined me as a business partner, actually asked to join me. I didn't ask them. In my second year of business, that began to slow, and I started thinking, *What do I do now? I'm going to have to share this opportunity with more people, and I have to be the one to do the asking.* And this is exactly what I did, but it occurred a good twelve months into my business, and it slowed my momentum. I should have been asking about and sharing the opportunity from day one.

What do you feel is the main reason you've succeeded in this industry while others haven't?

I stayed the course and never gave up, even when life occasionally got tough. I took my time, as it has never been a race for me. This industry requires you to be self motivated, strong, determined, and passionate. And sometimes we hit roadblocks in our business, just like in life. It's then up to us how we handle those roadblocks. Do we learn from them, push through, and come out the other side stronger, more focused and with a new sense of direction? Or do we let it defeat us? I always chose the first path. Oddly enough, when I think about this question I immediately see similarities to my previous craft.

This business and industry is a journey, and an individual one at that, just like labour. There are peaks and troughs, difficult times and exhilarating times, just like labour. Some people will reach their goals quickly, whilst others will take longer, just like labour. The one thing for certain for both network marketing and labour, is that in the end, something magical is created and continues to grow as long as we nurture it and never give up on it.

Malcolm Stevenson Forbes says it well:

"Diamonds are nothing more than chunks of coal that stuck to their jobs."

How did you develop the confidence to undertake this business opportunity, and what were your biggest fears when you first started?

I've always been a fairly confident person, especially when talking about something I knew well, like midwifery. However, like most people, I was incredibly nervous when I embarked on this business venture. I really knew nothing other than I loved our products. The thought of standing up in front of a roomful of people and talking about a business opportunity that I was just getting to know myself, frightened me to no end. I feared what people would think of me as being *that direct-selling lady.* I was worried that people would think, *Why is she doing this when she has a degree?* I was also concerned that no one would join me in my business, because I didn't really believe in myself as a business owner at first. I was afraid of failure, that it wouldn't work, and all of these people who looked at me like I was crazy for attempting the business, would be proven right.

I had to make a conscious decision that no matter what, I was going to give this business my all. Feel the fear and do it anyway. No matter what people said or did to deter me, I committed to myself that I would make this business work. And I did. I surrounded myself with positivity, chose to ignore the negative, and fed my mind with thoughts of success rather than failure.

First, I read everything I could about our products, the success plan, and the network marketing industry. I needed to be equipped with the knowledge to answer questions and show I was taking this little 'side venture' seriously. I immersed myself in the success stories and was relieved to hear about the vulnerabilities and doubts other leaders and mentors experienced in the beginning.

I showed up to every event my uplines, Angela and Debbie Loughnane, put on. Even though I couldn't see myself in the bigger picture of success like these two amazing women, I stole my belief from them and used their stories to inspire not only myself, but others as well. And although I was shaking in my boots, I regularly got up to share my story at these events, which built my confidence and further cemented my belief that I *could* do this business and succeed.

The proof came in having three business partners ask to join me in my first six weeks in the business. This categorically boosted my confidence and made me feel like maybe I did have something to offer, and maybe I could be as successful as my two incredible uplines, Angela and Debbie Loughnane.

Practice makes perfect in this industry. Confidence in talking to people about a network marketing opportunity only comes from doing it over and over again. Now I could say my business spiel in my sleep, and I'm just so excited to share this incredible gift with as many people who will listen, because it works, and it's a game changer. And because I'm so open to all possibilities now, on a daily basis I'm being asked that all-important and critical question.....ized"What do you do?"

You talk about how having your network marketing business has allowed you to expand your family. Now that you have four children, what does this mean to you and your husband?

My husband is one of four children himself, and it had always been our dream to have four children of our own. But financially, if I'd stayed in my midwifery job, it would have been a real stretch for us, and I wouldn't have been able to stay at home with our children. So to be able to have the choice and financial freedom to realise our dream of being a family of six, is absolutely priceless.

Ava and Ivy have never known me when I was involved in the shiftwork of midwifery life. They have their mum pretty much 24/7 and will never have to see me 'go to work' as such, because this business is not work. They watch me excitedly getting ready in the bathroom, and sometimes Ava, who's three, will say, "Are you going to a business presentation, Mum? Have fun." The business is part of our life and our family, and I still sit in awe sometimes as I walk our kids to school, watch them play at the park, and breastfeed our twenty month old any time I want to. Sometimes I wonder how I got so lucky.

What are your top five tips for success in the network marketing industry for someone who's just started?

1. MIND YOUR MIND.

   So much of the success in this industry comes down to mindset. It's so important to feed your mind with positivity and to think in possibility and abundance, rather than in limitation and negativity. Anyone can succeed in this industry as long as they have belief. Belief in themselves and belief in the product and business they're a part of.

   It's also really important to protect your mind from the comparison game. We may see others fly through the ranks of network marketing companies quickly, and it's easy to fall into the trap of saying, "Why is it not happening like that for me? What am I doing wrong?" The answer is, *Nothing*. Everyone's journey in this industry is different and individualised, which is what's so great about network marketing. We can all write our own story. Some will sprint through their businesses, while others will take more of the steady marathon approach like I did. Either way, you can build and grow a successful business as long as you keep your mind in check and focus on what drives you to do the business in the first place.

2. HAVE AN ACTION PLAN AND SET GOALS.

   Setting goals is such an integral part of making your business work and for growing a sustainable and viable asset. Goals keep you focused on growth and put you in good stead for longevity in the industry. We should never stop setting goals and targets for ourselves or our teams, because this industry is a collaborative effort of many. We need to set the example for our teams, so we can inspire and encourage them to be bigger and better and to DREAM BIG. I always write my goals down and break them into weekly, monthly, and yearly goals. Then I break them down into activities, with an action plan to match. This holds you accountable.

3. BECOME A COMMUNICATION EXPERT.

    Network marketing is all about building relationships with people, including consumers and business partners, and is solely based around that belly-to-belly relationship. That's why it's such a successful industry. So much of my residual income is derived from the wonderful relationships I've formed within my business. Therefore, being an effective communicator and listener goes a long way to remaining a success in the industry.

4. BE CONSISTENT.

    The key to success in this industry is not to go out and run yourself ragged every day. Rather, it's all about being consistent. By simply doing one income-producing activity for your business every day, you will set yourself on a path to success and will be creating good business habits. We often say you can do network marketing part-time but not some of the time. Set a routine for yourself and time block. Have set times each day or week you allocate to building your business. That consistency will ultimately lead to your lifelong success in the industry.

5. BE COMMITTED.

    Respect your business and the decision you've made by committing to it one- hundred percent. Lead by example and set the bar. You are the CEO of your own empire, so treat it like that. Plug in. Show up to all of the trainings and events on offer within your teams. Do some personal development every day. Declare your goals verbally to your friends and family and also write them down all over your house, so you can see them every day and be held accountable. Fill up your belief cup by listening to positive and successful leaders in your business who've paved that path, and steer clear of dream stealers. Don't be afraid to dream big and create the life of your design. I can promise you, it will be so worth it.

Sharon Wilkes

"Decide what you want. Believe you can have it. Believe you deserve it and believe it's possible for you."

Jack Canfield

CHAPTER FOURTEEN

Sharon Wilkes

What was your childhood like?

I'm the eldest of four girls and grew up in Country Victoria, where I enjoyed a wonderful childhood. I was an excellent student, a junior and senior state champion in Highland Dancing, played tennis and piano, had a small group of wonderful friends, and my life seemed on a consistent path where I would move to Melbourne for tertiary study and work as a finance professional.

That was, until I met my husband. Scott and I had a couple of classes together in Year 10 at high school, and we quickly became inseparable. We often look back and say that perhaps we just met each other ten years too early, but I'm a big believer in fate, so I think the universe had different plans.

A chain of events led to me to discovering I was pregnant at fifteen, which was an enormous shock to Scott, me, and our families. Although difficult at first, I was incredibly lucky to have the support of my family, and Scott instantly assumed responsibility as a father, which is in part credit to his upbringing and family support, as well as his strength of character. I still feel enormously blessed to have a husband who was able to take on such an incredible task and in many ways protect me from the opinions of the wider community, which were not always kind.

How did this turn of events change your lives?

Ultimately, the choice to have a baby at sixteen put both of our lives on a different course but one for which we're both enormously grateful.

Our beautiful baby girl, Bridget, was born at the end of my Year 11, which meant I had a few months to enjoy a new baby and then straight back to complete my Victorian Certificate of Education (VCE). To be honest, I had never considered doing anything else. Scott and I both felt instant responsibility for a brand-new human, and I always wanted to be completely self-sufficient. It was important for me to be able to stand on my own two feet and have a career. I never wanted to be reliant on anyone. I think this comes from my upbringing, as both my parents worked. My mum was a primary school teacher, and my dad owned an engineering business.

It was quite a shock to everyone when I became pregnant, as I really was, and I quote my mother here, "a model child." I never questioned authority, and with busy, working parents I was extremely responsible helping at home with my younger siblings.

Year 12 was challenging, but Scott and I used to walk Bridget to daycare each morning on the way to school and then pick her up on the way home. Scott spent as much time as he could with us, but he did live twenty minutes out of town and was also studying, so it wasn't easy. I was fortunate to have family support during this time, as well as a placid and healthy baby.

Scott and I both scored well in VCE and decided to move to Melbourne to continue our studies. Scott studied pharmacy, and I undertook a Bachelor of Business/Arts (Japanese). Bridget was fourteen months old, and Scott took her to daycare each morning on his way to Pharmacy College and picked her up in the evening. It's not easy to be responsible for a baby at any age, but looking back, I can say we didn't know any different, so we just got on with it.

It did impact our choices, as we were both keen to travel. I had wanted to remain in Melbourne as an accountant working at one of the Big Four accounting firms in order to launch my career, while Scott wanted to work as a pharmacist overseas. However, Scott returned to our hometown to complete his pharmacy experience, and I commuted four hours each way for my final year at university each week to see Scott and Bridget and stayed with Scott's family during the week.

After this challenging year, we remained in Swan Hill for one more year, and I worked a fulltime job at a local accounting firm before we moved to Horsham, where Scott was offered an opportunity to manage a pharmacy. We enjoyed five years in Horsham and were blessed with our second child, Lachlan. We again moved, this time to Geelong, as Scott was offered another opportunity to manage a pharmacy, and we also felt this would be great for our children, because it would offer a greater choice of education. It also meant being closer to Melbourne, where we both had family. We had a lovely home, two beautiful children, and great jobs. Life was comfortable, but I couldn't shake the feeling there was more to life.

How did you get into network marketing?

I was introduced to network marketing in 2011 at my friend's home and was impressed with the products being demonstrated. However, with Bridget going into VCE and me having started a new job in government, the business wasn't for me at that time. I did take another look in early 2013 after returning from a six-week family holiday to America. I'd been thinking about doing something else and spoke to Scott about how great it would be if we could keep travelling like this each year.

Network marketing prompted me to question what my life was going to look like in five years if I kept doing what I was doing. I had so many goals and dreams, and I realized I had to make a change if I wanted to achieve them. I really enjoyed my job as a taxation accountant, but I knew being an employee was not going to create the kind of wealth I wanted that would allow me to do what I'd dreamed about. I want to volunteer and help others less fortunate, and I wanted to spend time with my children and family when I wanted to, not just when I was told I could. Most importantly, I wanted to create the change to show others what is possible in their lives.

Scott was sceptical at first, but after further discussion, he kept an open mind, and we jumped in.

Who has inspired and influenced you, and why?

My parents were always open to new opportunities, and my father, in particular, loved to give everything a go. So I think I grew up with that mentality. They also encouraged me to spend time with people I admired and who were successful in what they did. By striving to do that, I always felt like I was moving forward and could dream bigger.

With both of my parents working, I always assumed I would do the same, and I'm grateful for their strong morals and hardworking mentality. I've always felt the need to be independent financially, and I strongly believe it's vital for women to have a sense of independence and not to be reliant on anyone, despite their circumstances and upbringing.

My parents also offered, and continue to offer, unwavering support in everything I've chosen to do in life, and I'm sure this support was critical in turning a seemingly difficult situation of being such a young mother, into a wonderful experience for us all. My parents recently celebrated their thirty-eighth wedding anniversary, and I'm so proud to have watched their relationship grow and be able to model my own relationships on their strength.

Scott has been a positive and motivating partner since we started our journey, and now that we've spent the majority of our lives together, I can say I'm so grateful we found each other, albeit early in our lives, and it's exciting to imagine the possibilities of what's yet to come. He's always worked so hard to provide a wonderful lifestyle and safe home for us all. Because he's fiercely protective and often sceptical, he provides a wonderful balance to my sometimes nonchalant, yet determined, attitude, and I love that we complement each other so beautifully. It's a joy and a pleasure to work alongside him in our network marketing business and grow together.

Our children, Bridget and Lachlan, inspire me every day to be the best version of myself, and watching them grow has taught me so much about the kind of person I am and the person I strive to become. It's so rewarding to have raised a child to adulthood with strong morals, beliefs, and goals to make a difference in the world.

My three sisters are my best friends, and we have so much fun together. Nothing makes me happier than when we're together with all of our families. having a ball. As the eldest, I've always felt like their protector, but now as adults, we support and love each other and have such a close bond, for which I'm forever grateful.

I'm blessed to call Chelsea Launer and Debbie Loughnane not only business partners, but friends. Their unwavering support is a constant source of motivation and inspiration.

I've also been blessed with wonderful employers and managers during my career in accounting, and many of them have been women, which has only fuelled my belief that women can be such amazing leaders. Networking marketing, and the incredible culture of our organization, has continued this experience seamlessly and further inspired my goal to be the best leader I can be.

When you were offered this business, what were your main concerns, and how did you overcome them?

I was never offered this business as such, but a leader in the industry had kept in touch with me after I began using the products. It wasn't until I returned from an overseas holiday with my family that I approached her to find out more about the business opportunity. I wanted to be able to take more overseas holidays with my family, and I knew that having a network marketing business could provide me with an additional income stream and create this opportunity.

Following my research, I felt the benefits of network marketing were abundantly clear. My main concern was having Scott's support. We've always made big decisions together, and I think we've always communicated, had similar goals, and headed in the same direction. This made it easier for me to show this opportunity to him. We both respect each other's goals and ambitions. Having said this, Scott was sceptical in the beginning and thought I was a little crazy, but he was open to the opportunity, and once he took a look at this business, he couldn't find a reason for me not to do it. He was so impressed, he decided to do it as well!

Another concern I had was how I was going to fit this around my work, family, and social commitments and still be able to create a successful business. My business partner, who introduced me to the company (my upline), explained to me how to find time around my current commitments by utilizing a weekly calendar where I would write down my work, family, and social commitments and highlight the times and days where I could work in my network marketing business. I've always been a busy person, and as they say, "Give something to a busy person, and they will get it done." Well, this was definitely the case for me. I quickly started to realize how I could easily work my business around the pockets of time I had throughout my day and plan out my week and month.

My final concern was that I didn't know enough people, so I got a blank piece of paper, put it on the kitchen table, and every time I thought of someone I knew, I wrote their name down. It's amazing to realise how many people you know when you really think about it, and it didn't take long to write down a hundred names. People would move off the list as I contacted them and come onto it each day as I met new people, whether professionally or socially.

Coming from the financial sector and being an accountant, you would understand the creation of a residual income and how important that can be for your retirement. Can you talk about how the network marketing industry also creates residual income and your opinion as to how that can help people?

Many people begin a network marketing business to satisfy all sorts of personal needs. For me it wasn't just for the extra income to travel, it was also for personal development and to meet new people. I love the discount on the products, and it wasn't until I continued to attend events that I really considered it for true wealth creation and to attain the time freedom I'd been lacking.

For many who are disenchanted with their careers, want to stay at home with their young family, or are nearing retirement and simply can't afford to retire, network marketing can provide a welcome answer. With a low-cost start-up, it's an attractive structure for people of all ages and backgrounds.

Make no mistake. Network marketing is not a get-rich-quick scheme, and when many people who start this business realize they're not making a six-figure income in the first few months, they give up. They forget that in a traditional job, an employee is constantly trading time for money and working to grow their employer's business. If they don't work, they don't get paid. This is what's so attractive about network marketing. Just by sharing the opportunity with others and teaching them to do the same, you're duplicating yourself and getting paid for the effort of everyone on your team. Leveraging is wonderful, and it's the basis of network marketing and the reason it can create such enormous wealth.

Having a financial background meant I understood this concept well and just had to share it with everyone. I've found it can be an advantage not having a background in the products you're sharing, as the people you're sharing it with can often relate. Network marketing can be for everyone. You don't need experience, you just need to be willing to learn, be passionate, and put in the work, especially at the start. If you treat it like a hobby, it won't pay you like a business.

It's also important to understand what you're actually selling. I was attracted to the products being consumable. I wasn't continually finding a new customer base but just looking after the ones I had whilst introducing them to new people. The great benefit is that over time, by duplicating your efforts, you can create an incredible organization for which you get remunerated, and the actual time you spend on your business becomes more and more about growing as a leader. I was really excited about the personal development, as even though I was not necessarily confident about everything when I started, I never stop growing as a business person, coach, friend, and leader.

You and your husband are both professional and educated people, so how have you two overcome the stigma of building a network marketing business?

After ten years of study between us, it was challenging to change from "I'm a taxation accountant" to "I own my own network marketing business." We both had to overcome our own personal stigma that we're professionals in our fields, and we own our own network marketing business. This is something we should be proud of.

Neither of us had really looked at doing anything else before, so it did take a little time to say to someone, "I own my network marketing business, and I'm an accountant" and not the other way around. In the beginning we would always lead by saying "I'm an accountant" or "I'm a pharmacist," and sometimes we didn't even say we owned a network marketing business at the beginning, because we were worried what people would think of us. We continue to come across those who have their preconceived ideas about network marketing. Most of the time this is because they've known someone who's had exposure to the industry, and they've imparted their feelings about the industry.

There were two strategies that helped us to overcome this stigma. The first has been to consistently spend time with successful network marketers and attend training events. It cemented in our minds that this was an incredible opportunity, one that deserved to be taken seriously, and of which we could be proud. Spending time with successful network marketers also helped me to quickly build a strong and resilient mindset and to respect that everyone is entitled to their own opinions around my decision to start my own network marketing business. It's okay if this business isn't for them, or they might not agree with the decision I've made. I learnt not to take it personally. If someone didn't want to do what I was doing, it wasn't because they didn't like me. It was because they couldn't see themselves doing what I'm doing at this point in their lives.

Secondly, spending ten to fifteen minutes per day on personal development has been a huge contributing factor in helping us build a strong, positive, and resilient mindset. This could be reading books, listening to audio books, or attending conferences.

What has been the biggest surprise to you on your journey in this industry?

Personal development and new friendships I've made.

It's something I would have never imagined this business opportunity would provide. Initially I knew the financial benefits, including the residual income, but never in a million years did I think I would receive some of the best personal development training and also meet and become friends with so many amazing women and men.

I've attended lots of conferences in my professional career as an accountant, but the personal development I've received in my network marketing business has been unbelievable, to say the least. I've consistently attended every available conference, training, coaching calls with my uplines, and audio training, as well as reading books recommended by my peers. It's all helped me to grow into a much stronger, happier, and confident woman. I've always felt these qualities within myself, but I've had so many people I know personally and professionally also make comments, which has been rewarding.

It has also helped me to become a stronger leader, so I can in turn help others to do the same. I feel I'm now able to better help people in big and small ways. This business has given me the confidence and courage to be willing to go out and try new things and not be scared or worried about what other people might think. I know I'm making a difference in people's lives, and I look forward to being able to continue to do so.

The friendships I've made already in my short journey have been gratifying. To be friends with likeminded, positive women and men who share the same vision has been fantastic. While I've only known these people for a relatively short period of time, I feel like we've been friends forever. I know this may sound corny, but to have people who are genuine and care about you as a person, and not because of who you are or what you might be able to do for them, is something to be treasured. We all need that wonderful support network in our lives, and this business opportunity has done just that.

What does your future look like now, because of network marketing?

Working as an employee, I was spending a lot of time with people who live from day to day, pay cheque to pay cheque, and who don't afford themselves the chance to dream about what could be. I noticed it the most when I started spending more and more time with successful people in the network marketing industry. They're happy, inspired, grateful, and full of possibility, which made such an incredible difference to how I began to view my own situation.

I know the business I've started, and continue to grow, will provide me and my family with so many amazing new opportunities in the future. One of the main reasons I started this business was to allow us to travel more, and in our first two and a half years in this business, we've travelled to the USA twice, the Gold Coast twice, Sydney, and Bali. I know if I hadn't started this business, we certainly wouldn't have travelled to at least half of these places, but because I was courageous enough to say yes, we have, and I look forward to all of the amazing places and countries to which we've yet to travel.

It excites me to know that the future in my business will give me the time freedom to choose what I want to do, when I want to do it. My perfect day will be waking up, going for a walk along the beach, having a breakfast and coffee overlooking the ocean, playing golf with my husband, enjoying spending time during the day with my family, sharing and helping others grow their business, and perhaps a little shopping! Before I started this business, I hoped my professional career would provide me this opportunity, but although I have financial freedom, I'm still trading time for money.

Network marketing offers a different model for creating that choice. Now I'm working to build my own business and create my own dreams, not helping to create someone else's. It will be gratifying in the future to give back to others. Having been a teenage parent, I'm really looking forward to starting a charity where I can help other teenage parents have the courage and confidence to know their future can look bright with the help of others. For them to know that having a baby at a young age doesn't mean they can't live the life they've always wanted. They can continue to follow their dreams.

What's your advice to someone who's looking at a network marketing business and thinks it's not a professional industry?

Be open to possibilities of what a network marketing business could provide you in your life. Imagine what your perfect day would look like. Dream big. Write down twenty things you would love to have in your life. They don't have to necessarily be materialistic, like a house on the beach or a red Ferrari, but they can be. For me it's to travel more, to have time freedom where I can choose to do what I want when I want, like spend more time with my family and friends, and to do more charitable work.

Then ask yourself, *Is what I'm doing now going to allow me to accomplish that within the next five years?* If not, then something has to change. Don't be one of those people who thinks, *I've been to university, earned a degree, and now have a professional career, so I could never start my own network marketing business, because it isn't professional enough for me.* In many cases you're making someone else rich and giving them what they want in life instead of yourself.

Don't be worried about what other people think of you. At the end of the day you're the one in control of your life. It's you who has to pay your bills. If people criticise you for starting your own network marketing business, don't take it personally. I know this can be hard to do at the start, especially if they're a loved one. Perhaps they're too scared to try this for themselves for fear of failure, or they may not want to see you succeed. The best you can do is prove them wrong.

Don't go through life thinking, *What if?* The great aspect about a network marketing business is that you don't have to invest a lot of money to set yourself up. You need some products, a phone, and a method of transport. You don't have to put your house on the line. You don't have to take out a massive loan. Have the courage to start your own business, as you never know where it might take you.

How do you work your network marketing business around your fulltime professional career as an accountant?

The majority of people who start a network marketing business do so around a fulltime job, whether as a paid employee or a fulltime, stay-at-home parent. I knew this business was flexible enough that I could fit it around the nooks and crannies of my day. It's vital to be organized and keep a calendar, as these tools will help you keep on track and ensure your allocated time is used effectively.

In the evening, I write down the top five income-producing activities I need to do the next day, work out the time I have available to do that, and lock it in.

It's also important to book in time for yourself and your family, as these are often the reasons we start a network marketing business in the first place: to give us back time with the ones we love.

My sister introduced me to NET time or *No extra time* several years ago, so I started making phone calls in the car, listening to personal development when I was out walking, and basically combining activities that I could do together. She also introduced me to Parkinson's Law, which is basically the concept that work expands to fill the time available for its completion. I love this, as I used to allocate three hours to clean my house, and that's exactly how long it took. Yet when I had guests arriving in an hour, I could pretty much do the same thing in a much shorter time period. I work to ensure my time is used as effectively and efficiently as possible. We all have the same 168 hours each week, and it's all about what we choose to do with them.

My absolute favourite people to work with in this business are those who have a lot going on in their lives, as they have fantastic organizational skills, juggle many tasks, and tend to get it all done. Again, it comes down to priority. We all have to juggle competing priorities in our lives, and we make those decisions every day. I might decide one morning I will sleep in rather than going to the gym, which is fine for one day, but if I make that decision every day, I will never achieve my fitness goals. The same goes for all of our decisions during the day. At the time a task may not seem that important or that it can wait, but really we're just delaying our own progress. Goals are just dreams until you give them a plan and a deadline.

Could you give five tips to people who are in network marketing or looking at joining a network marketing business?

1. DON'T FEEL YOU HAVE TO KNOW EVERYTHING AT THE START.

   Starting a network marketing business can feel unnatural to most of us. Why? Traditionally we're educated, and then we get a job. Network marketing is the opposite. We start our business and learn as we go. So don't feel you need to know everything at the start. If you consistently plug in to all of the training and coaching that's available to you, combined with activity, you will continue to be motivated to succeed in this business.

   The key word is consistency. Let's say we put it back to the traditional way of life of going to university first, and then getting a job. Do you think you'll pass your degree and get a job if you only turn up to university when you feel like it? No. Same applies to attending trainings available to you in your network marketing business.

2. FOLLOW THE SYSTEM

   You will no doubt have wonderful, experienced leaders from whom to learn. They've already made mistakes and learnt from them, so copy what they do, and don't try and reinvent the wheel.

3. IT DOESN'T MATTER WHAT BACKGROUND YOU'RE FROM. THIS BUSINESS IS FOR EVERYONE, SO NEVER JUDGE.

If you take the time to see what many leaders in the network marketing industry did prior to owning their business, you'd be surprised. There are accountants, pharmacists, lawyers, doctors, teachers, bank managers, and corporate executives, just to name a few. Keep an open mind. You never know who might be interested in this business. Everyone deserves the opportunity to take a look and see if this business might be for them. I've been surprised by people in this industry who've wanted to start their own business. I quickly learnt you can't pigeon box people and assume they will or won't be interested. No one knows what's going on in someone else's life, and this business opportunity could be exactly what they're looking for. Let them make the decision if this is something they're interested in or not. It might be just what they've been looking for.

4. IT'S YOUR JOURNEY, SO DON'T COMPARE YOURSELF TO OTHERS

When you start your business, don't worry about how quickly other people are growing their businesses. Stay focused and grow your own, keep consistently learning, and you will be successful. It doesn't matter what anyone else is doing, it's your journey, so enjoy it!

5. BELIEVE IN YOURSELF

This has been a huge attribute for me to develop, as I spent a long time in my comfort zone. I knew I was capable of more, but it's one thing to say and another to do. Work on yourself daily, because only you can make the change you desire. We're here for a good time, not a long time, so make every day count. You can do this!

"It ain't about how hard you hit. It's about how hard you can get hit and keep moving forward."

Rocky Balboa

CHAPTER 15

Tarnee Rowan

CHAPTER FIFTEEN

Tarnee Rowan

What is your background? What was your childhood like?

All of my life I've believed I was destined to change the world somehow. Little did I know it would be through owning my own network marketing business and changing lives one person at a time. My passion for seeing others smile, feel free, and be happy started from a young age. I love being able to help so many people from different walks of life achieve some of these feelings, as I didn't for a very long time.

From birth, I was diagnosed with a degenerating disease called Charcot Marie-Tooth, which causes the nerves and muscles to waste away. There's no cure for this hereditary disease, which is something I've learnt to deal with over the twenty-six years I've been alive. Growing up being so different from the kids at school was hard at times, especially when they would imitate me behind my back and pick me last in team sports. It used to make me feel alone and like I was the only one in the world feeling this way. I would put on a brave face and hide how it wasn't okay, but deep down I was hurting. I learnt to be the best actress and faked my smile when meeting new people, because I thought they were judging me on how I looked and walked.

Throughout my childhood and teenage years, I'd been in and out of hospital. I've had fifteen major surgeries on my feet, legs, and hips. This took its toll on me, and it came to a point where during my last surgery I went into heart failure and had to be brought back to life. This was the last straw. I took a stand and said "No more, mum. I've had enough. I'm done." I knew from that moment on in my life I was going to be a difference maker, and I would be the one to prove to everyone that I'm different, and nobody out there can stop me from creating greatness. I had to be the person who got knocked down, or in my case fell over continuously, but kept getting back up no matter what.

What were some of your early jobs?

I finished year 12 and worked in a large retail store while studying to become a personal carer for the aged. Aged care was a rewarding job but also took its toll on my body and was physically too hard for me. I followed my heart and became a beauty therapist. Making others feel good and look great is something I'm passionate about, but more importantly, I enjoyed educating men and women in these areas.

Working as a beauty therapist was great, but I couldn't leave the guests feeling as amazing as I wanted to, because in the position I was in, it involved long, exhausting hours and back-to-back massages while standing for hours on end. My heart began to fall out of love with where I was working, and I lost my passion. That's when I made a bold move to quit, with no job to fall back on.

How did you get into network marketing?

I had two options at this point. I was twenty four, freshly single, and looking into working on cruise ships to get away from everything and everyone. Or I could say yes to an opportunity that was presented to me by a fellow friend I'd met at beauty school, Jacquii Jackson, and start up my own network marketing business.

I'm so thankful now that I chose to spend such a small amount of money on a business rather than a plane ticket to the seven seas. I spent the first nine months with my head down, bum up in my business. I grew an enormous team of leaders, made lifelong friendships, found true love, retired myself as a beauty therapist this year, and get to live my life without an alarm. If I had to choose again, I'd absolutely say yes to starting up my own business.

Having a network marketing business teaches you so much about the world, yourself, and the people you're surrounded by. It assists you in broadening your skills in every aspect of your life.

At least it's done all of this for me. I was quite a shy, timid little girl who was afraid of what people thought of me. Until I got used to you, then it was hard to shut me up. I love that since becoming a network marketing professional,

I've gained so much confidence in myself to the point where other people's opinions of me don't matter, as I'm not their prisoner. I have the confidence to be who I am. I share all of my knowledge with everyone who's willing to receive what I love sharing.

I have the confidence to ask questions without being attached to the outcome and the possibility of rejection. All of this confidence is because of the organisation I'm proud to be a part of, the friends, leaders, and mentors I aspire to be like, and the personal development I choose to participate in, so I can grow myself.

Another aspect of network marketing I love is the friendships I form. I always found it hard to make new friends and was thrown into a situation as an insecure child moving from Melbourne, where all of my friends were, back to the small country town where I was born and knew only one person. I didn't have many friends growing up. Even in my early twenties, when I was surrounded by different people, I still felt as though most of them weren't true friends. I wound up asking on social media pages where to buy friendships. Little did I know putting that question out to the universe would allow me to buy into a business that comes with loads of new people who've become some of my very best friends.

Everyone isn't for network marketing, but network marketing is for everyone. I love that you don't have to go to university or study for years to learn how to be successful. And if you put your mind to it, get into action straight away, and learn as you go, then it can create the best life for anyone hungry for the success. As I said, I was a beauty therapist before my network marketing business allowed me to be financially free and retire. I can now work my own hours, wake up when I feel like, do as I wish on a daily basis, and never have to work another Boxing Day, Easter weekend, public holiday, or miss any of my niece or nephew's birthday's ever again. I don't have to worry if I'll run out of petrol, because my bank account is overdrawn the day after I've been paid.

I have so many more choices in my life and know I haven't even scratched the surface yet. To me, this is what it feels like to not only be financially free, but to be free from *the man*. The one who sits by the pool sipping on

mojitos with his $5,000 suit, because he brought a business that has millions of people working and slaving day in, day out, working public holidays, missing birthdays, weddings, holidays, family time, and making a life to remember in order to make him richer.

Working for yourself can seem like hard work, but the one thing I've learnt is that having a network marketing business means you're not in business alone. Unlike traditional retail businesses where you work your backside off to be successful and feel terribly alone, network marketing is much different. For me to have my own business where I can be coached and mentored for free by amazing leaders who've paved the way of success, I feel there isn't anything much better, really. Other than being able to pay it forward and teach those who join my team exactly what I've learnt and continue that on down the line to create great independent leaders.

I'm not saying it's been an easy and straight-and-narrow path to get to where I am now. There have been challenging hurdles, speed bumps, blockages, and a lot of fear that has gotten in the way. Like with everything, we all face challenges. It's how you deal with them, learn from how you handled the situation, and remember to keep moving forward.

One of the biggest hurdles I've faced so far in my business was believing others were judging who I was, and therefore it allowed me to cast judgment on others. This was a massive block in my business for quite some time, as I couldn't see it happening and just went on with my day-to-day business. Then I had a coaching call with my business mentor and leader, Emily, in which we talked about what was holding me back from moving forward in my business. I knew not only did I have to be honest with her, but in order to move forward I needed to be honest and raw with myself to get to the bottom of what was really going on. This is crucial for everyone in business to learn how to do.

There were a few issues that day I could mention, but the one that really stood out to me was judgment. I was holding back, because I thought others were judging me for not being blonde enough, or skinny enough, or that I didn't have the ability to wear fancy high shoes, or high shoes at all for that matter, or my clothes weren't fashionable. I came to realise nobody was judging me, and they were just thoughts I believed to be true. I was comparing myself to other successful leaders in the business.

This wasn't my only bit of judgment. I was judging other people's ability and making up their mind for them, before I had even asked them any questions. This meant I couldn't ask if someone wanted to join my business and be a part of our growing team, because I was making a judgment on them that they would say no to me, due to all of the thoughts that were going through my head about myself.

This was toxic thinking, and I'm so thankful I recognized it, so I could move forward. I had to do a lot of personal growth and development to get over this hurdle in order to get to where I am now. With the help of Emily, I was able to fill up my love cup by surrounding myself with positive, uplifting leaders, turn up to all events and trainings, and not miss a coaching call, online or in person. I've also been able to plug into different audios on Soundcloud from people in network marketing. I learnt to love myself, I was exercising every day, and building my confidence with how I looked and felt. I started to be proud of who I was and who I was turning into. I freed myself from drama, negative people, and toxic friendships that were constantly sending me around in the vicious cycle.

As I mentioned earlier, when I started up my business, I wasn't working in a salon, as I had left my fulltime job. But I was doing bits and pieces from home for family, friends, and referrals a few days a week. Having the flexibility and freedom to work my business however I chose right from the start, really appealed to me. I knew I could work as hard as I could and get to where I wanted to be super quickly, or I could just ease into it and prolong the process.

Within my first two months I was in the first level of management and kept up with massive amounts of activity. I reached my cash bonus, plus more, every month for quite some time. I built a team quickly and was working around the clock to see them succeed. This became hard work for me, as these people weren't meeting me halfway. They weren't willing to put in the time to practise the strategies for which I was coaching and mentoring.

I'd focused so hard on building up my team's businesses that I forgot about my own. And although they were all a part of my team, my personal activity was non-existent. I was in over my head with debt and needed right-now money, so I found work in a hairdressing salon and began as a beauty therapist there.

How were you able to incorporate your network marketing business into your beauty therapist position?

While offering new treatments to the salon, I made a promise to myself that my business would still always come first and that I'd continue to grow while working at my job. I came into contact with lots of different clients, day in and day out.

At the beginning, I was afraid to ask them if they would be open to trying samples or watching a presentation about what I was doing, but then as I grew as a person, gained my confidence, and plugged in to different types of personal development, I realised I was casting judgment on the people I was meeting and deciding through my own made-up reasons, that this business or products wouldn't be for them.

That isn't my judgment to make. So every person I met, I spoke to them about the business and related it back to how network marketing could fit into their busy schedule, help pay for family holidays, upgrade their car that wasn't mechanically sound, and all of the other benefits that come along with the small start-up cost. I stopped holding back and saw massive changes within myself as a person, beauty therapist, and friend. I didn't have to work around my busy schedule or make calls during my lunch breaks, because I was able to do all of this from the comfort of the beauty room, as well as on my days off by just building relationships with clients and allowing them to trust me in the process. Having a business built from friendships and trust are two of my most absolute necessities, as without them, it would be complicated and hard work.

Do you have any mentors? Who inspires you?

Throughout my life I've always been inspired by successful and fun people and looked up to them, because I wanted to surround myself in their company and soak up who they are. Some of the people who inspire me the most are the following:

My mum and dad.

Leanne and Rick, who would both give the clothes off their backs to see my brother, Troy, and I succeed in life. They're two of the most giving, loving, caring people I know and have been the ones who always will have the biggest part of my heart. Making me into who I am today and always encouraging my brother and me to be our best selves by doing whatever it is we desire to do. I thank them both from the bottom of my heart for always believing in me. I will never stop loving them both for all that they are and all they do for me.

My brother, Troy

Right from the first moment I can remember, he's always had my back. Growing up together we may have had our fair share of fights, but the love I have for him and his family has just grown more and more each day. I'm so thankful to have a brother like him who no matter what, is always there for those he cares about. Especially his wife, Shelley, and his two children, Mia and Xavier. He may not know it, but he's always been one of the big reasons why I'm so strong now and don't take any crap from people, as that's how I always viewed him and wanted to be that same. I appreciate him much for always being my bro.

My True Love, Darren.

He came into my life when I wasn't looking for anything serious, and I'm so thankful he did. He's the most generous, kind, loving person I've ever come across. He supports me in any decision I make that will make me happy. I learn from him every day, but most importantly I love him more and more every day. This is something I never thought would be possible to do again. I feel as though I'm the luckiest girl in the world to have him as my partner in crime, best friend, and love of my life.

My Sponsor, Jacquii Jackson

The moment I met her at beauty school I felt a sense of peace. She inspired me to join network marketing and give something new a go, but she also inspired me to see who I truly was as a person and evolve into something much greater than I could ever dream of becoming. I'm always thankful for her friendship, but even more thankful she had the courage to ask me to join her team and trust in me that I would be a team member she could count on to see it through.

My uplines, Emily and Debbie Loughnane

These amazing women continue to inspire me every day. And without this business, I never would have had the privilege to know them as well as I do.

Emily is one of the main reasons for how great my life is now, and how I'm still here today smiling with confidence. The way she leads and coaches her teams, builds friendships, and drives her business with every ounce of her being, while continually managing to make it about everyone else, proves to me what she's willing to do to see other people in her life as happy as she appears to be. She's one in a million, and I'm so thankful to have a friend like her in my life, inspiring me every day and paving the way for Gen Y's and everyone else out there.

Debbie's courage to stay the course and build an entire organisation who all aspire to be just like her, is something she should be so proud of. She's changed thousands of lives, including my own, just by saying yes and creating something so unique.

I have to thank them both so much for kicking my bum when needed but also being my support.

My team.

For believing in me and saying yes. Every day I'm faced with a challenge in this business and overcome it with ease for them. I learn so much from them all and am so inspired by who they all are as people for many different reasons. I wake up every morning pinching myself, because I'm surrounded by the best people in the world and am lucky enough to call them my business partners but also lifelong friends.

I wouldn't have become the leader I am today without any of them or their ever-growing teams. I appreciate them challenging me, for their belief in me, but most of all I appreciate them for allowing me to be present in their lives. Love to Samantha Dobbin, Katrina Vosper, Jamie-Lee Clohesy, Shelley Rowan, Yazmina Alder, Georgie Murrell, and to their extending teams. And to all those who've come and gone, I thank them all as well, for teaching me much more than they could ever imagine.

What do you love most about the network marketing business?

The biggest gift I've received being in this industry, would have to be financial freedom. As I mentioned briefly, I was in over my head and had quite a bit debt myself. I owed people money all over the place, as I was struggling to live week to week. My pay cheque would come in for the fortnight and before I could even put the essentials in the pantry and fridge, the money was gone. I was living with a friend of mine at the time and relying on friends and family to feed me on different nights of the week. This went on for quite some time.

Monday was leftovers from Sunday's roast dinners, Tuesdays were cheap pizza night, Wednesday was family tea at an ex-friend's, Thursday was snatch and grab, Friday was whatever I could afford, and Saturday I often went without. This wasn't an ideal lifestyle and wasn't the life I'd seen for myself, so when I became financially free and started having more money coming in than going out, I felt a massive shift within myself. I no longer felt sick at night wondering if I would make it to see my parents who lived half an hour away, due to having no petrol or money. I didn't have to worry about putting back the roast chicken a few days before Christmas, because my card declined and I was having everyone over for Christmas lunch.

There was a massive weight that lifted from my shoulders that had been weighing me down for several years. I truly felt free. As my income kept increasing, I knew that one day I would have much more money than I would know what to do with. And this is when I found a real reason to be in a network marketing business with a residual income that continues to grow monthly. My *why* became so big that it started to make me dream again. And for me, this meant I could finally give back.

What would you do differently if you had the chance to go back and do it all over again?

If I had to go back and restart my business again, I wouldn't do anything differently. Everything I've done in my business has taught me valuable lessons about how to handle different people and situations and enabled me to grow into the person I am today, because of all of the objections, rejections, complications, setbacks, and hurdles I've had to face.

Although if I knew then what I know now, there's no way I would hold back on offering this opportunity to everyone I came into contact with, while the excitement and fire in my belly from starting a new business was fresh in my mind. Over time, for some reason we tend to put a spin on situations and complicate them a little bit. Then we need to process what we're about to face, decide if it's going to be something that will be in our comfort zone or way out of our comfort zone, and then our mind just says, "Nope," and in the too-hard basket it goes.

If I were to restart my business, I would not let any of these silly little problems affect me. I would just go in with my heart and soul and take my mind out of the equation while I built my business. This is how I approach everything that comes my way now. I believe you're in the best position when you first start, as nobody expects you to be great straight away, because you're not supposed to know everything. People join you in the excitement of your vision. But the thing is, as long as you can clearly paint a vision of where you're headed and what's in store with pure excitement, people will still be attracted to that, no matter how long you've been in business or what title you obtain.

What rewards have you gotten from your network marketing business?

I've been in the industry now for two and a half years, and I must say that no other industry rewards and recognises the efforts of their leaders like they do in network marketing. What I've been personally recognised for so far has just blown me away but also been the driving force to want more for myself and give the gift to others to feel the same.

Two months after joining, I was rewarded with gifts and a voucher to spend in my personal shop for meeting certain requirements. In those same months, I was also promoted to the first level of management. I've been recognised for promoting out two team members to the same level of management as myself, which was one of my biggest achievements and the most rewarding so far. Being able to see others' lives change for the better brings me pure joy and happiness. In August this year I was one of fourteen who earnt an all-expenses paid retreat for a beautiful night away. To earn this, I had to be at the second level of management and become an area manager, which I had done well before the qualification period ended.

Why did you choose network marketing?

When I first looked into network marketing and the company's philosophy, I thought it sounded too good to be true. I also had a preconceived idea of what the network marketing industry was like and didn't want to be seen as a diploma-qualified beauty therapist who had to resort to a pyramid scheme, because she couldn't find work or was too lazy for a nine-to-five job.

I pondered in my thoughts before trying the products, as I'm a yes person and knew once I tried the products I would feel guilty and have to say yes even if I didn't want to. I did some Google researching and found mixed reviews about the company and the industry. But in my heart I just had that feeling this could what I needed in my life. Before knowing too much about it, I couldn't stop thinking about it.

Then when I was willing to trial the core range, it was instant love at first touch, smell, and sight. The products felt amazing on my sensitive skin. I'd been a beauty therapist who was never able to practise what I preached, because I couldn't wash my face or use products on my skin without it causing a reaction. They smelt almost edible and were safe for my skin, as there were no nasty chemicals or fragrances for a reaction to be caused. I wasn't able to fault these products and was hooked when I saw the results within twenty-four hours. After my first experience with the products I could tell they were worthy of being in salons all over the world, and I believe it will be in the near future. It's that good.

What do you see in your future?

In the future I have hopes to open a program for younger kids to feel connected to the world. I want to teach the younger generations it's okay, and they can grow up to be whatever they wish to and be that living proof of inspiration for the ones who don't have anyone to look up to. I also want to be able to make enough money to see my parents retired and living out the dreams they always dreamt of but could never afford. I want to give back to them after all they've given me, even when there was nothing left to give.

I feel as though I have a grasp on my life and can feel there's no limit to what will be created in my future. But I do know that because of the opportunity of network marketing, I will have a lifetime of choices to live my life truly as I wish. I can clearly see how bright my future looks and love that this opportunity will allow me to do everything I've ever dreamt of, such as travelling the world. I used to have a list of countries I'd love to visit and how long I'd spend in each place.

I would love to fulfil that wish one day soon and enjoy it with people I love spending time with, which I know is possible within this industry. As I said, I can see myself expanding out into different places with programs for kids with disabilities who don't feel valued and worthy. I'd love to be able to teach them what I've learnt and how I've become the person I am today.

Most importantly I know for sure I will continue to help as many people reach their goals as I can and teach them to stretch their dreams, just like my mentors have done for me. I want to help them reach for the stars, and then stretch even further and be proud of the achievements.

I always want to pay it forward with no recognition or rewards back in return. Smiling is infectious, and I intend to make the world smile with me and become a place where we can all be happy, free, and feel loved by those with whom we're surrounded.

What are your top five tips for those aspiring to get into network marketing?

My top five tips for aspiring GEN Y's to succeed in network marketing would be the following:

1. SPEND THIRTY MINUTES EACH DAY PLUGGING IN AND DEVELOPING YOUR SKILLS.

   Read as much as you can and learn about the industry for when those tricky questions arise, so you can become the network marketing professional you can truly be. By plugging in, you'll also learn to grow and become the person you aspire to be. When you develop yourself on a personal level, the world seems like a much nicer place, as you've learnt to let go of your ego and come from the heart. This is exactly what all successful leaders in network marketing do.

2. LISTEN WITH BOTH EARS OPEN, EYES CLEAR, AND MIND SWITCHED ON.

   Always ask questions if you don't know the answer or you're unsure, because chances are someone else has been in your position. No question is too big, too small, too silly, or too intelligent.

   But when asking, make sure you're willing to hear the answers, even when they may not be what you want to hear. Be willing to soak up all there is to learn from the different leaders who've paved the way and are proven to be successful in network marketing. It works best not only from word of mouth but in duplication. The leaders before you have tested out what works, what doesn't, and how to simplify everything you may be overcomplicating. Go back to basics and start fresh like you know nothing and have to learn it all over again.

3. IF YOU'RE NEW TO NETWORK MARKETING, BE SURE TO WRITE DOWN HOW YOU'RE FEELING.

   I know when I first started I was feeling overexcited, a little scared, determined to succeed, and prove a few toxic people wrong. I was also proud of myself for making a decision that could ultimately change my life, as well as many other people's lives around me. Then when you're feeling a little low in your business, go back to that book and remember how you were feeling. Read it over and over again, until you begin to believe the feeling is yours, and no hurdle to big or small can change the way you first felt when you joined the network marketing industry. Keep the excitement alive, share the opportunity you have with everyone, and let them know it's easy to jump in head first without the knowledge, and even easier to learn the rest later.

4. EVERYTHING THAT'S GOING TO HAPPEN IN YOUR LIFE AND BUSINESS, HAPPENS FOR A REASON.

We all choose the pathways we'd like to lead down and follow. Those setbacks, numerous amounts of rejection, and negative and toxic people, are easy to overlook if you stay in your own personal activity and build your business, regardless of what's happening around you. Stay focused on where you're heading, and those negative vibes won't matter to you. There will come a point when you'll look back and be able to laugh at how silly they were, even if it seemed terrible at the time. Everything is always fixed with a full calendar of activity, so go for the gold, and don't hold back.

5. BUILD YOUR BUSINESS SO BIG EACH MONTH, IT'S LIKE YOU'RE STARTING OVER AND OVER WITH A CLEAN SLATE.

Not only will you be successful super quickly, but this will teach you to stay in personal activity and not sit back and reap the rewards from your teams, who are out there doing the work you've been training and coaching them to do. And if you miss a bonus or promotion because you slacked off for the month and let your team do the work for you, then you have nobody to blame but yourself. I guarantee if you do slack off, your team will know, and they will stop doing what they're doing until you lift your game and be their inspiration.

Be the living proof. Prove to yourself you're good enough to do this. Prove to the naysayers that network marketing is a growing industry, and you're not going to be left behind in the next big wave of professionals.

Prove to the company you choose that you're in it for life, through thick and thin, fun and tears, and enjoy the journey by keeping it simple and having fun along the way.

Be the living proof. Prove to yourself you're good enough to do this. Prove to the naysayers that network marketing is a growing industry, and you're not going to be left behind in the next big wave of professionals. Prove to the company you choose that you're in it for life, through thick and thin, fun and tears, and enjoy the journey by keeping it simple and having fun along the way.

Conclusion

After spending hours interviewing these wonderful women, I was left with a sense of awe, and a belief that this world is full of great people who've faced challenges and still find the courage to rise above it to do great work. I hope you've received this book's central message: love yourself, and be a catalyst for change. Follow your dreams, and give yourself permission to shine.

Just by altering your perception and believing in yourself like these women did, you can, and will, make a positive difference to those around you.

> *I have learned over the years that when one's mind is made up, this diminishes fear; knowing what must be done does away with fear.*
> ### Rosa Parks

> *Pretty women wonder where my secret lies, I'm not cute or built to suit a fashion models size.*
> *But when I start to tell them, They think I'm telling lies,*
> *I say,*
> *It's in the reach of my arms,*
> *The span of my hips,*
> *The stride of my steps,*
> *The curl of my lips*
> *I'm a woman*
> *Phenomenally.*
> *Phenomenal woman*
> *That's me"*
> ### Maya Angelou

You are a phenomenal woman, go on and unleash your brilliance.

With love and gratitude.

Nkandu

About The Author

Nkandu Beltz

2015 Africa Pioneer of the Year Award, 2014 Women in Leadership Award, 2013 Creative Innovation Scholarship Winner, 2012 Young Social Pioneer. Author of I Have The Power Book. Author of Fierce and Fabulous - The Feminine Force of Success Book. Engaging Speaker and Master of Ceremonies.

Nkandu Beltz is the Founder and Chief Empowerment Officer of Fierce and Fabulous. Nkandu is an author, philanthropist, social change maker, and lover of humanity who has worked in the not-for-profit sector for over ten years.

Born in Zambia, she now calls Australia home. Nkandu is devoted to making a lasting change and to help people live a better life. She initially started out as a girl child advocate, advocating for equal rights and raising awareness regarding HIV/Aids.

She has a background in journalism and news writing and has work for Ngami Times in Botswana and Warringarri Aboriginal Radio Station in Kununurra in Western Australia. She later became an Australian Youth Representative to the Commonwealth Heads of Governments meeting in 2011 She was chosen as Young Social Pioneer in 2012 by the Foundation For Young Australians.

Nkandu is passionate about youth development, creating community, and helping others. She has worked with Save the Children Australia and was an Executive Member for the United Nations Association, Western Australia.

Nkandu is a 2013 Creative Scholarship winner and is an ambassador and mentor for STEMSEL (Science, Technology, Engineering, Mathematics and Social Enterprise Learning).

She is also the only Young Social Pioneer to interview His Holiness the Dalai Lama. Nkandu comes with a wealth of knowledge, life experience, community, and connections. She has a strong bond with young women and men across Australia and is in touch with issues facing young people, particularly in smaller to remote country areas.

Resources

Download free *I Have The Power* from

www.ihavethepowerbook.com

www.nkandubeltz.com.au

www.fierceandfabulous.com.au

FierceandFabulous.com.au

Other books by Nkandu Beltz

I Have the Power

Welcome to the tear-jerking and uplifting life story of a social change-maker and humanitarian: Nkandu Beltz. In her first published book, *I Have The Power,* Nkandu shares her entire story from being born as a 'girl child' in Zambia through to her life here in Australia today.

By recounting her adversities, including being poisoned, as well as the many extraordinary experiences she has been blessed to have in life like interviewing the Dalai Lama, Nkandu aims to inspire every reader to realize that they DO have the power to change the world.

A book that stays with you long after you read it, *I Have the Power* is set to inspire people around the world to find *their* own amazing journey and make a difference to the lives of others.

Emily Gowor

Author, Publisher, and Speaker

Fierce and Fabulous - The Feminine Force of Success

"With every experience, you alone are painting your own canvas, thought by thought, choice by choice."

Oprah Winfrey

"Our deepest fear is not that we are inadequate, our deepest fear is that we are powerful beyond measure...We ask ourselves, who am I to be brilliant, gorgeous, talented and fabulous?"

Marianne Williamson

"Never underestimate what an individual with a powerful thought can do!"

Nkandu Beltz

Fierce and Fabulous shares the reality of what it means for women in business today, and how adversity can become a driving force for business, community, and change.

- Are you a woman who wants more?

- Are you searching for success?

- Is your life running on love or fear?

In this book, we have a deeper conversation with women about:

- the real issues women in business are facing

- how to go from Struggle Street to Success Avenue

- how to overcame adversities so you can live your dreams.

YOU ARE Extraordinary!

Fierce and Fabulous is a dedication to the lives and achievements of extraordinary women who are changing the world. This is a collection of the stories of inspirational women.

Featuring: Chantal Harris, Eva Sifis, Fauza Beltz, Fur Wale, Gaye O'Brien, Jacinta Petrie, Kelly Fletcher, Kia Dowell, Philippa Ross, Rebecca McIntyre, Sharron Keating, Suzanne Waldron, Tania de Jong, Therese Howell, Rebecca McIntyre and Yeukai Ota.

Nkandu Beltz is an author, speaker, change maker, and philanthropist. She has a background in journalism and news writing. She has interviewed His Holiness the Dalai Lama and other extraordinary leaders.

Fierce and Fabulous Diaries

Have you ever wondered how some people seem to succeed at everything they do? We want to help you find their mission and clear your vision to live an inspired life. We are dedicated to helping you live the best life you can.

The women featured in this book are highly skilled at what they do.

You can sign up for workshops around the country on various topics, as well as hear more about these fierce and fabulous women through webinars and podcasts.

As the architect of Fierce & Fabulous, I hope you will join me on this inspirational journey by becoming a part of our community and creating an environment for the next generation to flourish and thrive.

You might want to purchase one of our inspirational, limited-edition Fierce and Fabulous diaries.

For more details, send an email to admin@nkandubeltz.com.au or visit us at www.fierceandfabulous.com.au.

Want to be a Published Author?

Writing and publishing your very own book does not have to be hard. You just need to have a message to share.

At Author Express we love to turn your publishing dreams into a reality. If you are;

- *A Difference-Maker* - People that have a message they want to share to make a difference in the world

- *A Business Owner* -The best business card on the planet is a book

- *A Writer* – You've written your book and just want to know the most effective way to publish it, then we would love to help.

To find out how you can *Share Your Message, Make a Difference and Leave a Legacy* ™ simply go to www.AuthorExpress.com

Author Express

From Inspiration To Publication In 5 Simple Steps

www.ingramcontent.com/pod-product-compliance
Lightning Source LLC
Chambersburg PA
CBHW060242220326
41598CB00027B/4010